GORSUCH

THE JUDGE WHO SPEAKS FOR HIMSELF

JOHN GREENYA

THRESHOLD EDITIONS

New York London Toronto Sydney New Delhi

Threshold Editions
An Imprint of Simon & Schuster, Inc.
1230 Avenue of the Americas
New York, NY 10020

First Threshold Editions hardcover edition January 2018

THRESHOLD EDITIONS and colophon are trademarks of Simon & Schuster, Inc.

For information about special discounts for bulk purchases, please contact Simon & Schuster Special Sales at 1-866-506-1949 or business@simonandschuster.com.

The Simon & Schuster Speakers Bureau can bring authors to your live event. For more information, or to book an event, contact the Simon & Schuster Speakers Bureau at 1-866-248-3049 or visit our website at www.simonspeakers.com.

Interior design by Bryden Spevak

Manufactured in the United States of America

10 9 8 7 6 5 4 3 2 1

Library of Congress Cataloging-in-Publication Data.

Names: Greenya, John, author.
Title: Gorsuch : the judge who speaks for himself / John Greenya.
Description: New York : Threshold Editions, 2018.
Identifiers: LCCN 2017044174 (print) | LCCN 2017045010 (ebook) | ISBN 9781501180385 (eBook) | ISBN 9781501180378 (hardback)
Subjects: LCSH: Gorsuch, Neil M. (Neil McGill), 1967- | United States. Supreme Court—Biography. | Judges—United States—Biography. | BISAC: BIOGRAPHY & AUTOBIOGRAPHY / Lawyers & Judges. | BIOGRAPHY & AUTOBIOGRAPHY / Political. | BIOGRAPHY & AUTOBIOGRAPHY / General.
Classification: LCC KF8745.G67 (ebook) | LCC KF8745.G67 G74 2018 (print) | DDC 347.73/2634 [B] —dc23
LC record available at https://lccn.loc.gov/2017044174

ISBN 978-1-5011-8037-8
ISBN 978-1-5011-8038-5 (ebook)

To Chris

To the memory of Jim Greenya, Mike Greenya,
and Denise Del Priore Greenya.
R.I.P.

I WOULD ALSO LIKE TO CLARIFY

—NOBODY SPEAKS FOR ME.

NOBODY.

I DON'T HAVE SPOKESMEN.

I'M A JUDGE. I SPEAK FOR MYSELF.

—*Judge Neil Gorsuch, before the Senate Judiciary Committee, March 21, 2017*

Contents

Introduction

At exactly two minutes past 8:00 p.m. on January 31, 2017, in the East Room of the White House, Donald J. Trump presented the nation with Neil McGill Gorsuch of Colorado, the person he had selected to fill the United States Supreme Court seat left vacant by the sudden death of Antonin Scalia on February 13, 2016.

One of the most unusual aspects of the ceremony was that the name of the nominee had not leaked and spoiled the surprise. In the early days of the young administration, most of Trump's choices, especially those of his cabinet members, had been leaked. Not this one. The important secret had been kept, and then revealed with all the deft theatricality of a finale on *The Apprentice*.

On Monday the thirtieth, Trump had phoned Gorsuch and told him he was his nominee. Trump's eventual list of twenty-one had gone down to six, four, and then two before Neil Gorsuch became the president's pick.

The physical route by which the forty-nine-year-old jurist and his wife, Louise, had made it to Washington for the Big Reveal had been cleverly concealed from the media. After he got the call from Trump on Monday telling him he was the nominee, the judge and his wife went to the house of a friend who also lived in Boulder.

There they were met by several lawyers from the office of the White House Counsel who briefed Gorsuch on how the next night's ceremony would go down.

After the briefing, Judge and Mrs. Gorsuch were driven—by a circuitous, back-roads route—to the Denver airport where they boarded a military jet for the flight to Joint Base Andrews, just outside Washington. In D.C. they spent Monday night at the home of friends, where they were picked up the next day and driven to the White House.

Later that same day, Press Secretary Sean Spicer told reporters, "You saw a very well planned out and well-executed strategy tonight. This was a great effort by the entire team."

The reactions to the president's nominee from both sides of the political aisle were immediate and predictable. Senator Charles Grassley, the chairman of the Senate Judiciary Committee, said Gorsuch was "an extraordinary judge," but Senate Minority Leader Chuck Schumer called him an "ideologue." Massachusetts senator Elizabeth Warren, a Democrat, and Nan Aron, president of the progressive Alliance for Justice, used the same word—"disastrous"—to describe the Gorsuch nomination.

Given the relatively recent history of battles over nominees to the Supreme Court, such disparity of views should come as no surprise. This time, however, the Democrats were, understandably, still furious over the fact that the Republicans, in a move that had Democrats screaming "Foul," had blocked the confirmation of Judge Merrick Garland, then-president Obama's choice to fill the Scalia seat. Never before in American judicial history had this happened, and the wound was still raw.

★

ACCORDING TO SENATOR SCHUMER (D–NY), Judge Gorsuch "owe[d] it to the American people to provide an inkling of what kind of justice he would be." The minority leader may have *wished* that Neil Gorsuch felt he owed that duty to the American people, but if he had, it would have gone against decades and decades of actual practice.

In 1993—twenty-two years before the confirmation hearings of Chief Justice John ("I call balls and strikes") Roberts, no less a liberal icon than Ruth Bader Ginsburg told an interviewer, in an oft-quoted statement in the pre–"going viral" era, that she would give "no hints, no forecasts, no previews." One commentator wrote that Gorsuch "proved an especially ardent follower of what has come to be known as the Ginsburg rule."

In the six-week period between the nomination and the beginning of the confirmation hearings on March 20, Gorsuch began the charm offensive, visits to senators' offices so they could take his measure to help them decide how to vote on his nomination. Even though they knew better (or should have), many senators used the occasion of these visits to ask Gorsuch how he would rule on specific cases or issues.

Neil Gorsuch is a tall, pleasant-looking man with strong features, a full head of prematurely gray hair, and a trim physique. While answering questions or reading his statement, he sat up straight, as if posing early for Mount Rushmore. The morning after the hearings opened, a *Washington Post* story headlined "Supreme Court Nominee Neil Gorsuch's First Day of Hearings" featured glowing assessments from Republicans and vows of further scrutiny from Democrats.

"Gorsuch," it said, "steered clear of controversy," and "tried to reassure senators he was a mainstream jurist who was in the majority in 99 percent of the 10 years of cases he decided on the appeals court. Gorsuch said he has ruled 'for disabled students, prisoners, undocumented immigrants, the rich and poor, and against such persons, too. But my decisions have never reflected a judgment about the people before me—only my best judgment about the law and facts at issue in each particular case.'"

At forty-nine, Neil Gorsuch has a commanding presence. While delivering his thirteen-minute statement in a firm voice and with a resolute manner, he even *looked* western. The conservative columnist Charles Krauthammer agreed: In a panel discussion on Fox News' *Special Report*, several days before the hearings began, Krauthammer said, of Gorsuch, "This guy's out of central casting. This is a Gary Cooper character. Attacking him is a losing proposition."

Gorsuch may not, like the late movie star, say "Yup," but he is given to expressions that make him sound older than his forty-nine years. On the day after Gorsuch gave his opening statement, Dana Milbank, the *Washington Post*'s sometimes snarky but never dull political columnist, wrote: "The nomination of Neil Gorsuch presents the Senate with a constitutional dilemma: Is this nation prepared to have Eddie Haskell serving a lifetime appointment on the Supreme Court?" Eddie Haskell is the "Golly, gee-whiz, Mrs. Cleaver" character from the television show *Leave It to Beaver*.

That Neil Gorsuch speaks like an older person and uses terms that make him sound retro compared to his contemporaries is not surprising to those who have known him for a long time. Dr. Steven Ochs, who has taught advanced placement history at Georgetown Prep for four decades and was faculty advisor to the student council the year Gorsuch was senior class president, recalls, "There is a way in which Neil *always* was older, or seemed older, than his age, even back then. He was more involved in and knowledgeable about the political issues of the day than the others in his class."

Another surprising distinction is that, in contrast to her son, Neil's mother, the late Anne Gorsuch Burford (she divorced Neil's father, David Gorsuch, in 1982 and married Robert Burford the following year), was known for her colorful use of language, making her what reporters call "good copy."

In agreeing to step down as head of the Environmental Protection Agency, she did so only after negotiating a promise that once the dust had settled she would be offered a position of comparable status in the Reagan administration. But when that offer turned out to be for a seat on the Advisory Committee on Oceans and Atmosphere, she told the press she had turned it down because the job was a "nothing-burger." (That term was seldom heard after Burford left Washington, but it resurfaced in the presidential campaign of 2017 when Hillary Clinton used it to describe her emails problem.)

Two elements made the Gorsuch hearings seem surreal. One was extraneous to the proceedings, and the other absolutely central to their outcome.

The first was the fact that while his nominee was fielding questions with aplomb, the president of the United States was having a tumultuous, volatile first one hundred days, which made everything he put forward marked by opposition and requiring a fight for passage.

The second element, the more central one, was that many observers, from court experts to men and women on the street, viewed the whole Judiciary Committee hearings as an exercise in frustration, because the Democrats did not have the votes to block the Gorsuch nomination. Or, if they somehow got them, Senate Majority Leader Mitch McConnell (R-KY), the man who'd kept his party from even considering President Obama's nominee Merrick Garland, had promised he would change the rules so that a simple majority vote—not a sixty-vote "supermajority"—would be sufficient to approve the nomination.

Sixty votes was the way it had been until the second term of the Obama presidency, when, in 2013, then–Majority Leader Harry Reid (D-NV) started the Senate down this slippery slope by changing the rules so that any judicial nominee—*except* for Supreme Court nominations—could be approved by a simple majority vote.

On Thursday, April 6, 2017, McConnell, faced with the strong possibility of a Schumer-led filibuster, made good on his threat to employ the nuclear option, and the fight was over. The United States Senate was changed, perhaps forever; Neil Gorsuch, the new Supreme Court associate justice as of that date, was not changed, and certainly was not damaged. With all the verbiage stripped away, the Democrats' essential problem with Gorsuch was that he was not Merrick Garland (which raises the question, did they expect Donald Trump to name a mainstream, middle-of-the-road candidate?), and it was time to move on.

DURING HIS CONFIRMATION HEARINGS, Gorsuch had been asked many questions, but the ones he refused to answer (à la Ruth Bader Ginsburg) all had to do with how he would vote on important hot-button issues of the day, which meant that the committee, the Court, and the country were left with three vital questions: Who is Neil Gorsuch? What kind of man is he? What can we expect of him as a Supreme Court justice? As Senator Mazie Hirono said to him during the hearings, "We need to know what's in your heart."

In order to learn that, one must look at where he has been.

Chapter One

A WESTERN CHILDHOOD

Neil Gorsuch's Colorado roots are as important to him as any other element of his history. While they may not be the deepest, in that his father's family originally came from Ohio and his mother's mother was from Nebraska (Anne, the judge's mother, was born in Casper, Wyoming, one of seven children), they are still deep. While he was growing up in Denver's Hilltop neighborhood, all four of his grandparents were alive, and—as he said in his statement before the Senate Judiciary Committee—"I could ride my bike to their homes and they were huge influences."

Going back several generations, the judge's family history on each side contains both doctors and lawyers. His maternal grandfather, Joseph John McGill, was a surgeon, and his father's father was also a medical doctor. Dr. Gorsuch, who lost his father at age four, grew up to become famously hardworking, putting himself through medical school by driving a Denver streetcar.

It was, however, Neil's paternal grandfather who was most deeply connected to, and well-known in, the city of Denver. Born there in 1899, John Gorsuch practiced law in that city until his death in 1987, becoming well liked and well respected. In a 2004 tribute in *The Colorado Lawyer* magazine, Ben S. Aisenberg, a partner and friend, called John Gorsuch his mentor, partner, friend, and "one of the most down-to-earth individuals you could ever expect to meet.

He could relate to people at every level. . . . He also was gregarious, soft-spoken, thoughtful, and humorous [and] so popular and well known in Denver that, during the '30s, '40s, '50s, and '60s, he could not take a stroll down Seventeenth Street at lunchtime without being stopped every few minutes by fellow attorneys, clients, or friends."

According to Aisenberg, John Gorsuch "served in the Armed Services in World War I. He loved to tell the story of being raised to the exalted rank of acting corporal. However, it was not long before he was returned to the rank of private when his First Sergeant informed him that he had not shown the qualities of leadership required of a corporal. John would finish the story with, 'Nuf said.'"

John Gorsuch, a skilled dispute-settler, was in great demand as an arbitrator of disagreements between management and labor unions. One of his favorite cases, writes Aisenberg, involved unhappy cocktail waitresses who were made to pay for their work wear, which consisted of tiny, revealing outfits and cowboy boots.

"The casino," wrote Aisenberg, "took the position that because the waitresses could wear their boots and skimpy outfits anywhere, it shouldn't have to pay for them. The waitresses maintained that they would not be caught dead in these clothes outside the casino and, therefore, such outfits should be considered uniforms and should be paid for by the casino. It was a three-day hearing, and the union paraded cocktail waitress after cocktail waitress in their revealing outfits to testify before John. He admitted he had difficulty taking notes during some of this testimony and was eternally thankful there was a reporter present who transcribed the proceeding." (Unfortunately, Aisenberg did not supply the outcome of the case.)

ALSO PROUD TO CLAIM a connection to the new Supreme Court justice is the tiny city of Leadville, Colorado (pop. 2,602), which bills itself, in contrast to Denver, as "The Two Mile High City" (10,532 feet above sea level). That connection is based on the fact that Neil Gorsuch's paternal grandfather, as the principal arbitrator for Climax Molybdenum, made many trips to Leadville for hearings, using the Loveland Pass, a high mountain pass—11,990 feet above sea level— in the Rocky Mountains of north-central Colorado, a journey that could be hazardous in the winter.

As the local newspaper boasted, "[For] those living in Leadville today, Gorsuch's appointment brings a renewed sense of civic pride that a man being named to the highest court in the land, has a connection to the highest city in [the] land: Leadville, Colorado."

★

AS FOR LAWYERS IN the family, in addition to grandfather John Gorsuch, both Anne and David Gorsuch, Neil's parents, were attorneys. They met in law school at the University of Colorado and married upon graduating. Only twenty when she finished her legal training, Anne had to wait until her next birthday to be eligible to take the Colorado bar exam; when she passed, she became the youngest person ever to be admitted to the Colorado bar. While they waited, the newlyweds took advantage of her having been awarded a Fulbright Scholarship to travel to Jaipur, India, where Anne studied criminal law.

Shortly after the president nominated Gorsuch, the *Washington Post* assigned a small team of reporters (three to report and write the story and two for additional research) to produce an in-depth profile of the nominee. The lengthy and informative article ran on the front page on Sunday, February 19.

According to the *Post*, "Gorsuch's parents . . . raised their three children on the art of verbal sparring." J. J. Gorsuch, Neil's younger brother, told the reporters, "When you expose, at an early age, children to the McLaughlin Group, you see people debating using their critical reasoning. . . . You come to the realization that there isn't just one side or the other that is right. The truth is often in the middle."

The *Post* reported further that "[in] grade school, [Neil] Gorsuch stood out because of this skill at quickly taking positions and backing them up. 'Other kids were not able to do this,' said classmate Gina Carbone. . . . He was definitely more mature than the rest of us, better informed and more advanced.'

"Another classmate, Rob Tengler, said, 'He wouldn't offer his opinion unless he was asked, but then he always had a whole lot more to say than the rest of us.'

"At the small private school Gorsuch attended, Christ the King Roman Catholic School, teachers drilled into their students the values of character, duty and service. While many students brushed off the moral lessons, Gorsuch seemed to internalize them."

Apparently, this trait stayed with Neil Gorsuch when he reached Georgetown Prep, the next stage of his education. In a phone interview for this book, Dr. Steven Ochs, who mentored Gorsuch in his senior year when Neil was student government president, recalled, "That year there was a religion teacher who wanted the students to debate *Humanae Vitae*, Pope Paul VI's controversial 1968 encyclical that, among other things, reaffirmed the Catholic Church's traditional position on the sanctity of life and the prohibition of contraception and abortion.

"No one wanted to defend it, including Neil, but he *volunteered* to defend it—and got a 96, the highest grade in the class. In effect, he had to defend 'the other side,' and he did that really well. There's a reason why Neil was a national debate champion."

In several places, the long *Washington Post* article made the point that Neil Gorsuch is not as doctrinaire as many people, especially many Republicans, seem to think, and the article ends by mentioning that back in Boulder, Judge Gorsuch and his wife are members of an Episcopalian church, St. John's, that is definitely not a conservative parish. Conservative groups like the Heritage Foundation went so far as to vet Gorsuch's *church* because it gets its parishioners from the largely liberal population in Boulder. In fact, it calls itself a liberal congregation, and advertised on its website for the Women's March on Washington. Nonetheless, the Heritage Foundation decided his attendance there was not a strike against him.

St. John's pastor, Reverend Susan W. Springer, told the *Post*, regarding Neil Gorsuch, "I am privileged to have spent enough time with the family to come to know Neil as a broad-thinking man, one eager to listen and learn, and one thoughtful in speaking. Those foundational qualities are ones I would pray that all public servants in a leadership role in our country might possess."

IN 1976, WHEN A group of Republican lawyers came to the Gorsuch home hoping to recruit David to run for the Colorado House, Anne told them, "You've got the wrong Gorsuch." Just weeks later, Neil Gorsuch, all of nine years old, was going door-to-door with his mother as she ran for and won a seat in the Colorado state legislature.

Before going to Washington, Anne McGill Gorsuch had worked at First National Bank of Denver, and then for three years as an assistant district attorney (for Jefferson County) for the City of Denver, a job she shared with another attorney named Ann, Ann Allott, today an immigration lawyer in Centennial, Colorado. Next, Anne worked for two state regulatory agencies, and then from 1975 to 1981 as a lawyer for Mountain Bell, the telephone company, taking a leave of absence to attend the annual legislative sessions.

In the Colorado House, Anne was part of a group labeled "the House Crazies," because of their passionate devotion to states' rights and their equally passionate opposition to the federal government's environmental and energy policies, a view that Neil Gorsuch's most conservative backers hope he shares. In the first of her two terms she was named outstanding freshman legislator.

David Gorsuch, Neil's father, joined his father's law firm upon graduation, and became a well-known labor lawyer, usually representing workers rather than management. According to the couple's friend Jim Sanderson, a Denver attorney who helped Anne get appointed head of EPA, David was a liberal, unlike his wife, who was becoming increasingly conservative, and these differences intensified as they began their marriage and their work as young lawyers. Mr. Sanderson, who later advised Anne, and who would have gone to work for her as the number-three person at EPA until the media raised what Anne considered a baseless conflict-of-interest issue, continued to advise her.

★

Neil Gorsuch's idyllic western childhood ended with his mother's appointment as head of the Environmental Protection Agency. She brought him with her to Washington, and, after what Jim Sanderson recalls was a lot of effort on Anne's part, he became a boarding student at Georgetown Prep, the prestigious Jesuit school in the D.C. suburb of Bethesda, Maryland.

Chapter Two

A FINE EDUCATION

Founded in 1789, the same year as Georgetown University, and originally located adjacent to it in the northwest quadrant of Washington, D.C., Georgetown Prep has a well-earned reputation as one of the finest high school–level educational institutions in the country. Among its famous alumni, in addition to Neil Gorsuch, are the poet Allen Tate; American actors John Barrymore (perhaps better known today as the grandfather of Drew Barrymore), Ian Harding, and Dylan Baker; former U.S. senator Chris Dodd; activist Anthony Shriver and his brother Mark; comedian, journalist, and writer Mo Rocca; William Bidwill, owner of the Arizona Cardinals of the NFL, and his son Michael, the team's president; and Brian Cashman, the general manager of the New York Yankees.

According to the school's website, "The highly structured curriculum emphasized study of the classics as a means of disciplining the mind, imbibing the wisdom of the ancients, and developing eloquentia or facility in speaking and writing. Students received a considerable amount of individual attention from their teachers and prefects, whose lives revolved around them. . . .

"Over the years, Georgetown Prep prospered because of dedicated administrators, teachers, prefects, talented students and great good fortune. Even in the face of adversity or changing currents within American society, it displayed remarkable resilience and adaptability; all the while remaining true to its essential principles—principles grounded in the spiritual insights of St. Ignatius Loyola. . . . As a Catholic school, Georgetown Prep helps young men to grow in their faith and understanding of the teachings of the Church and to learn to put their faith into action in the service of others. We welcome students of all faiths, believing that conscious reflection on one's faith, whatever it may be, leads to spiritual maturity and a commitment to serve others."

NEIL GORSUCH'S MOTHER WAS miffed because Georgetown Prep took its time in deciding to admit him. One night, before Neil was accepted, Anne attended a function at the school. A Jesuit priest was explaining to her, a bit condescendingly, that they might not have room for Neil because they had so many applications from sons of important people, such as ambassadors of foreign countries. Anne took that in for a moment, and then asked, "Father, don't you think it's time you buy American?"

The priest, realizing he had met his match, replied, "Mrs. Burford, we will accept your son."

WHEN NEIL GORSUCH ARRIVED at Georgetown Prep in the fall of 1981, it was one of those times of "changing currents within American society." Ronald Reagan was in the first of his eight years as president, and feelings pro- and con-Reagan ran high. Neil, his mother's son and political legatee, was a devoted Reaganite, which put him at odds with some of his new classmates who were equally devoted liberals.

Dr. Steven Ochs recalls, "Today we're about 490 students, and back then maybe 360. I had known Neil because he was in student government before he was president of the yard, and I was struck by how articulate and bright he was, and how informed he was, politically. Of course, as a history teacher that was a big interest of mine, and so we got along well. He was, as I said, very articulate and someone who could defend a position, but somebody who was very friendly, too, a nice guy. When we worked together on student government matters, he did a very good job of organizing. He's a very organized person."

The longtime history teacher also noticed, even back then, a quality in Gorsuch that others have commented upon over the years: "He's a good listener, and because he listens to people he's a very good leader. But he can also be authoritative—not authoritarian, but authoritative. He did a very good job here."

Georgetown Prep's Thomas Conlan, who also teaches history, but mainly economics, and who has been at the school about as long as Steve Ochs, taught religion when Neil Gorsuch was a senior, and was the faculty member who assigned *Humanae Vitae* as a debate topic. He agrees with Ochs's recollection that nobody, Gorsuch included, wanted to defend the controversial encyclical.

"I was trying to get somebody to defend it, and was thinking I'd have to throw in some extra incentives, because it was an unpopular position among everybody at the time, including the clergy. But Neil's hand rocketed right up.

"At that time I didn't know how good he was because I wasn't the debate moderator, and I didn't realize that he'd missed a lot of school that year because he was on the team. In fact, he missed graduation because he was at the Lincoln-Douglas debates, which he won."

Conlan recalls, "In defending *Humanae Vitae*, he really did a terrific job, even though at the time I'm sure I didn't agree with him. He was just so convincing, and a thorough preparer. His terrific articulation of his views was just so much better than anybody else's that I gave him the highest grade ever for *all* the senior classes—a 96. When he puts his mind to an issue he could sell snow to the Eskimos, as we used to say.

"He got along very well with the other students. There was some antagonism to his conservative views, but he was quite agile in defending them, and the classes were interesting because of that."

Tom Conlan remembers that Neil was good friends with both Brian Cashman, today the general manager of the New York Yankees, and also John Caldwell, who was Neil's running mate for the class presidency. "Caldwell," says Conlan, "was a good athlete—track and I think soccer, who went on to Notre Dame. As for Neil Gorsuch, he was a big winner here. Everybody loved him."

Dr. Ochs recalls being struck by Gorsuch arguing "passionately" with classmates over issues, including political topics, without getting angry. "He has a wonderful ability—and I think this came out in the hearings—to separate his personal feelings and look at things in a very dispassionate and objective way and, as in the case of *Humanae Vitae*, make the best case for the other side. He always had that wonderful ability to be dispassionate and to look at the other side.

"He was a *big* Reagan person, and of course his mom was this formidable Republican, and he made no bones about his political views. Now Prep is a pretty conservative place, but there definitely were also some liberals in Neil's class, and he would argue with his friends and they would really go at it, and then he'd say, 'Let's go get a hamburger.' He's stayed in touch with his classmates, and many of them are good friends today, like Billy Healy, who's a big, big Democrat, and William Hughes, a big contributor to the Democratic Party, who organized the big letter-writing campaign for members of Neil's class to support his nomination, pointing out how Gorsuch had always been able to maintain these friendships and disagree without being disagreeable."

IN THE TIME PERIOD between the nomination and the beginning of the Judiciary Committee hearings, there were media accounts that while he was a student at Georgetown Prep, Neil Gorsuch had founded a "Young Fascists Club." Dr. Ochs, who was quoted in several articles debunking the charge, explains what really happened: "There was a very liberal religion teacher at the school back then, and he would go at it with Neil in class, but in a friendly, joking way, and one day, after one of these exchanges, he said, 'Oh, you're all members of the Young Fascists League.'

"So, in the senor yearbook, Neil wrote, about himself, 'President and Founder of the Young Fascists League.' And when some of the media got hold of that, they started fulminating, and blah, blah, blah. But if you look back at it, a lot of kids made up fictitious organizations for the yearbook—we don't allow that anymore but we did back then—and the whole thing was a good-humored joke."

Even before he got to Georgetown Prep, Neil Gorsuch had shown signs that he took things more seriously than his peers. As the *Washington Post* reported in its lengthy February 19 front-page story, when Gorsuch was in grade school, the "Roman Catholic teachers drilled into their students the values of character, duty and service. While many students brushed off the moral lessons, Gorsuch seemed to internalize them."

Jonathan Brody, one of his closest childhood friends, said one incident in particular has stayed with him. When they were about twelve years old, Gorsuch borrowed a sleeping bag, and it got damaged or dirty in his care. He grew distraught.

"He was very concerned and upset that his honor and integrity would be questioned," recalled Brody, now a state district court judge in Idaho. "I remember thinking, 'Maybe I'm missing something. Do I not take this sort of thing seriously enough? Maybe I should.'"

NEIL GORSUCH BEGAN PREP school with everything going for him. He'd been accepted at a prestigious institution, and his mother was about to be named to a cabinet-level position in the administration of Ronald Reagan, a man young Neil admired greatly. The future looked bright for both mother and son.

For him, as he finished his first year and began his second, he knew he was in the right place. He and the Jesuit school were a good fit. For his mother, unfortunately, the story went off script.

First, her confirmation was held up for months by Democrats who questioned her qualifications to head the twelve-year-old agency that was charged with protecting Americans by protecting their air, water, and land. And then, about a year into her tenure at the Environmental Protection Agency, she got into a major brawl with Congress.

As was characteristic of Anne McGill Gorsuch Burford, acting out of loyalty to her boss, the president of the United States, she resisted the subpoenas of two House committees, one chaired by Representative Elliott Levitas of Georgia and the other by the powerful John Dingell of Michigan, both Democrats (the House was then under Democratic control). With the great benefit of hindsight, it's clear that she would have been better off had she worried less about protecting the president and more about protecting herself.

Burford's mandate from Reagan had three parts: reduce the number of regulations (and turn much of the watchdog responsibility back to the states); shrink the size of the agency; and cut its budget, a policy view strikingly similar to that of the current administration in 2017. As that approach to governance was what she had favored and fought for as a legislator in Colorado, she went at these tasks happily and agreeably. But fed by a media that was often hostile to Reagan, especially in regard to environmental issues, the perception of what she was doing—on the part of almost all the leading environmental protection groups—was that her real intention was to emasculate the regulations and protect the big polluters.

With easy access to both of the Washington and all the major East Coast newspapers and media, her oldest child was well aware of the swirling forces.

For decades since, the prevailing view in the media has been that Anne Burford had messed up at the EPA, and that early reporting was picked up and repeated by some writers at the time of her son's nomination to the Supreme Court.

For example, in late February 2017 in an article in *Newsweek* titled "Neil Gorsuch's Late Mother Almost Annihilated the EPA. Is History Repeating Itself?" Joanna Brenner wrote that Anne Gorsuch "was seen by some as a dictatorial 'Ice Queen' who wants to roll back Federal environmental regulations. . . . In addition to her surly disposition and budget slashing, Gorsuch was involved in a nasty scandal involving political manipulation, fund mismanagement, perjury and destruction of subpoenaed documents, among other things."

Despite the implication, the perjury charge was brought against an EPA subordinate, not Burford. In a 2017 *Washington Post* article titled "Neil Gorsuch's Mother Once Ran the EPA. It Didn't Go Well," Brady Dennis and Chris Mooney wrote:

While Anne Gorsuch might have suffered from a lack of diplomatic skills, she did not lack in personality and toughness. The *Post* once described her as "a striking woman with jet-black hair" who had "television star looks and perfect manicures.

She wore fur coats and smoked two packs of Marlboros a day; her government-issued car got about 15 miles per gallon of gasoline." The *Post* once wrote, "She could charm opponents, but she also did not shy away from political combat. Denver's *Rocky Mountain News* once said, 'She could kick a bear to death with her bare feet.'" [For a carefully documented view of Anne Burford's side of this debate, see *Are You Tough Enough?*, published by McGraw-Hill in 1986.]

In sync with this dusty opinion is the *Washington Post* report, also on February 1, 2017, that "her short, tumultuous tenure was marked by sharp budget cuts, rifts with career EPA employees, a steep decline in cases filed against polluters and a scandal over the mismanagement of the Superfund cleanup program."

GEORGETOWN PREP CLASSMATE THAD Ficarra remembers asking Neil Gorsuch, "How's your mom doing?" He said Gorsuch smiled and said, "She's doing fine, thank you." "It wasn't a brush-off," Ficarra told a reporter in 2017. "'Just so you know, your mom is in my prayers.' He said, 'I really appreciate that.' He was grateful for the support, but he didn't wallow in it."

As young Neil Gorsuch, who spoke to his mother regularly on the phone, and in person on occasion, was well aware, from the start of the Reagan administration the White House had been sparring with Congress over the concept of executive privilege, and when two House committees began to look into EPA's Superfund program, the White House and its lawyers, thanks to good soldier Burford, had the confrontation they wanted.

At the time she was asked to perform this service for the White House, Anne Burford did not know that two other Reagan administration officials who'd previously been asked by White House lawyers to fight this same fight had thought it over and said thanks but no thanks. One of them was Attorney General William French Smith, and the other was Burford's friend from Colorado, James Watt, the secretary of the interior.

When the White House lawyers came to Burford in the fall of 1982, they did not tell her their request had already been denied by the two cabinet members. And Watt, like Anne a true conservative soldier for Reagan, had been on the verge of saying yes when White House counsel Fred Fielding revealed something that made Jim Watt change his mind. Fielding said, "I just came from a meeting with Chairman Dingell and we may have reached a compromise that may be of value to us."

"What did that relate to?" asked Watt.

Fielding replied, "The general got into a situation similar to the one you are in, and we didn't want to create any embarrassment for the general, so we gave them the paperwork."

"What general?" said Watt.

Fielding, who had what Jim Watt recalled as "a scowl on his face like I was stupid," said, "The *attorney* general."

Watt said, "*Fred Fielding!* You're telling me that the attorney general had a case similar to mine, and the principle on which you marched me to the end of the plank is not important enough for him to stand on. But it's important enough for me to stand on and get abused like

I've been abused?" To which the White House lawyer said, "That's the way it goes, Jim."

Watt was able to get out of the executive privilege fight, but before that happened he and his wife were invited to attend a function at the White House. In an interview with this author for *Are You Tough Enough?*, Watt said, "But one night, while my fight was still going on, my wife and I were in the receiving line at the White House, and the president said to my wife, 'I appreciate what your husband is doing for me, and I want you to know that I will visit him every Thursday night if he goes to jail.' We had a big laugh about it. It was funny. I had a commitment: if the president wants me to do this, I'll walk the plank. But when they sold the principle down the river for the 'general,' I would not tolerate it any more. If the president asked me to walk the plank, I would have done it just like Anne did. But the president wasn't briefed on the truth of the whole situation."

EARLY ON, THE MEDIA caught the scent of scandal in the Superfund program, and it soon became a frequent and popular subject, with Anne Burford, the outspoken, attractive, and *female* head of EPA, as the focal point of their stories. To most of the press, Burford was refusing congressional requests for documents because she had something to hide. What they didn't know, because as a good soldier for Reagan she would not tell them, was that the truth was quite different.

From the outset, Burford had been in favor of giving Congress what it wanted to see (and had discussed this option with her oldest child), but the White House lawyers were so gung ho about preserving the doctrine of executive privilege that they were adamantly refusing her proposals to cooperate with the congressional committees chaired by John Dingell and Elliott Levitas.

Of those lawyers, she later wrote, "The people at Justice behind the push for executive privilege were all presidential appointees who, to be blunt, shared several characteristics: (1) they didn't have enough to do; (2) they weren't very good lawyers; and (3) they had tremendous egos."

So the issue was joined, the battles ensued, and Burford, who wanted to cooperate with Congress and get back to running the EPA, was getting clobbered in the media daily, none of which was lost on Neil.

At one point, she met with John Dingell in an attempt to talk him out of holding her in contempt of Congress for not giving up the papers, and pleaded, "Don't do this, John. If you do this it's going to end up like a Greek tragedy," to which the congressman replied, "Anne, you're right. It is going to be tragic. You know I'm not after you. You're just in the way. What you need to do is figure out who your friends are—whether they're up here, or at the other end of Pennsylvania Avenue."

Burford's reply: "I had to make that decision a long time ago, and I can't reverse it now."

"Well," said Dingell, "then you'll have to live with the consequences." Which is exactly what happened.

WHILE ALL OF THIS political frenzy was occurring, Neil Gorsuch was aware of his mother's woes, which became his, but internalized.

IN MARCH 1983, THE ax that had been hovering over Anne Burford's neck for so long began to fall, and on the fourth, after Burford had given a speech in Denver, she and her good friend Frieda Poundstone and Steve Durham, EPA's western regional administrator, were relaxing in Anne's motel room when Durham asked if he could speak to her "in private." Annoyed that he would not say what he had to say in the presence of Poundstone, she walked into the bathroom. He followed and closed the door.

"Joe wants to see you," he said.

Burford, who knew only two "Joes" in Denver, one of them being her father, figured the Joe well enough known in the city to be called by just his first name was Joe Coors, and she was right. He wanted to meet with her the next morning in his home, where she had never been before. Even though it was 3:00 a.m. in Washington, she called John Daniel and told him to write a chronology of all the events in her fight with Congress and get on the next plane to Denver.

As Burford later recalled: "The next morning, when they were in the privacy of his home office, the beer baron, eschewing small talk, blurted out, 'They want you to resign.'"

"They, who are 'they'?" It was all she could think of to say.

"People very close to the president."

"But why are you doing their dirty work for them?"

With a half-smile he said, "I never could refuse Ronnie anything."

Thinking quickly, Anne Burford said, "What's in it for me, Joe? What do I get out of it?"

"You get out," replied Coors.

"That's not good enough. Six months ago I tried to get an appointment with the president to offer to step down after the first two years of my term. But I was never able to get in to see him for that purpose. That 'get out' deal would have been fine six months ago, but not now. It's not enough."

"What do you want?"

For some reason she had the answer ready. "I want three things:

I want my people, the people I hired, taken care of—no wholesale firings; I want my legal bills paid; and I want a reappointment to a decent post in this term of this administration."

He said, "I'll make sure you get all three of those things."

When Burford got back to the car, she looked at her watch. The meeting had taken less than half an hour.

In the middle of this long-running drama, a reporter from the *Washington Post* called Georgetown Prep and tried to reach Neil Gorsuch "to get his side of the story." When Anne complained to the reporter's editor, he asked the reporter about it, and she claimed— either forgetting or unaware that the headmaster had taken her call and jotted down her request—that Neil had called her. As Burford quickly pointed out, seeing that her son's political views were a mirror image of her own, if Neil had in fact wanted to call a newspaper "to get out his side of the story," it definitely would not have been the *Washington Post.*

In the unlikely event that Neil Gorsuch had talked to a reporter, he undoubtedly would not have answered any questions about his feelings, but he might have mentioned what he told his mother when she phoned to tell him she was resigning as the head of EPA. As Anne later wrote, "Neil got very upset. Halfway through Georgetown Prep, and smart as a whip, Neil knew from the beginning of the seriousness of my problems. . . . 'You should never have resigned,' he said firmly. 'You didn't do anything wrong. You only did what the President ordered. Why are you quitting? You raised me not to be a quitter. Why are you a quitter?' He was very upset."

In 2017, the *Washington Post* reported, "[The] traumatic experience didn't derail Gorsuch. He became a national champion in debating.

And it didn't sour him on politics. Instead," said the newspaper, "it made him shrewder and more determined."

★

WHEN NEIL GORSUCH ARRIVED on the campus of Columbia University in the fall of 1985, he needed to be both shrewd and determined, because there were major differences between the Ivy League university in Morningside Heights in Upper Manhattan and the Jesuit prep school in Bethesda, Maryland, where he'd been cosseted for four productive years. At Columbia, even though almost two decades had passed, aftershocks of the famous 1968 riots were still being felt.

In the spring of that epochal year, students had protested against the war in Vietnam and the university's treatment of its neighbors, many of whom were middle- to low-income blacks. There had been a mix of liberals and conservatives in the student body at Georgetown Prep, but at Columbia in 1985 conservatives were few and far between. Nonetheless, young Gorsuch did not hide or temper his views.

Beginning in his first year, he contributed articles and opinion pieces to the student newspaper, the *Columbia Daily Spectator*. In one he called the student demonstrations "rites of spring" and in another wrote somewhat disparagingly of protests over such issues as a fraternity's treatment of women and black students, opining that they "inspire no one and offer no fresh ideas or important notions." But he did join a fraternity himself, Phi Gamma Delta. One former classmate took issue with his opinion that the protests "inspired no one." A February 5, 2017, Associated Press article quoted Andrea Miller, the president of the National Institute of Reproductive Health and a Columbia graduate who had edited the *Daily Spectator*'s opinion page, which ran contributions by Neil Gorsuch. Miller told the AP, "Racial justice and freedom of speech and sexual assault and misogynistic behavior at frats, those were burning issues, and they remain burning issues to this day."

That same AP story began with these words: "As a conservative student at Columbia University in the mid-1980s, future Supreme Court nominee Neil Gorsuch was a political odd man out, and he was determined to speak up. 'It is not fashionable at Columbia to be anything other than a pro-Sandinista, anti-Reagan protester,' the then-sophomore wrote in a campus newspaper. . . . 'Only in an atmosphere where all voices are heard, where all moral standards are openly and honestly discussed and debated, can the truth emerge.' In his college writings, Gorsuch took on many of the most controversial issues of the day."

Another Columbian who differed with Gorsuch was Jordan Kushner of Minneapolis, then a student activist and now a civil rights lawyer. According to Kushner, while the *Federalist Paper*—a campus newspaper founded by Gorsuch and two like-minded friends, Andrew Levy and P. T. Waters—may have been centrist, Neil Gorsuch was not.

"He's good at sounding reasonable," Kushner told the Associated Press, "but . . . he took really right-wing positions" on the issues on which the two disagreed, such as the Reagan administration's secret funding—using money raised by selling arms to Iran—of the Nicaragua rebels in their fight against the Marxist Sandinista government.

The prevailing sentiment on Columbia's campus was to oppose the administration's actions, but, as he had done at Georgetown Prep, Neil Gorsuch stuck up for President Reagan, defending him in the Iran-Contra matter (though he did fault him for being "indecisive"). Among other hot-button issues during the mid to late 1980s were: whether universities like Columbia should divest their holdings in businesses in South Africa (Gorsuch said the cause was "unquestionably an honorable one," but warned that divesting could have a negative impact on scholarships and the school's endowment fund); whether because of their antigay policies the military branches should be barred from recruiting on campus (Gorsuch defended their presence on the grounds of the First Amendment's free speech guarantees); and whether Columbia's curriculum should include more female and minority authors (Gorsuch: "If possible, yes").

AT THE TIME OF his 2017 confirmation hearings, in answer to the request of the Judiciary Committee for a list of his writings, Gorsuch went all the way back to college. As the *Denver Post* reported, "Gorsuch's writings include some made while editor of *The Morningside Review*, a quarterly journal of opinion published by students at Columbia University and founded in 1982. It was launched partly to give a voice to conservatives and moderates on campus, said one editorial. The publication was described by former Gov. Mario Cuomo as harboring 'stone-age conservatives.'"

In one article, Gorsuch attacked the U.S. State Department's handling of Afghanistan. Gorsuch, a Denver native, also coauthored a piece lashing out at those who joined that period's boycott of Coors beer over its relations with unions and minority groups.

In 2002, while in private practice, Gorsuch wrote an editorial for United Press International in which he said that in today's judicial confirmation process, "[There] are too many who are concerned less with promoting the best public servants and more with enforcing litmus tests and locating 'stealth candidates' who are perceived as likely to advance favored political causes once on the bench."

In 1986, newly graduated Gorsuch reflected on the *Federalist Paper* in another writer's *Spectator* article about conservatives on campus.

"I'm not sure that conservatism and Columbia can be easily connected," Gorsuch said. "However, the debate has been opened up considerably, and this is good."

He, along with his fellow *Federalist* editors, said something similar—and prescient—a year later. As reported by *Politico* in 2017: "Gorsuch and his fellow *Federalist* editors seemingly anticipated future scrutiny of their collegiate work in a *Federalist* editorial from November 1987. Following the failed presidential candidacy of Joe Biden after plagiarism allegations and the derailed Supreme Court nomination of Douglas Ginsburg for previously smoking marijuana with his students, the *Federalist* wrote that many students 'are coming to the realization that one's actions in college and one's conduct as a young adult will be examined in relentless detail should one chose [*sic*] to enter the public sector.'

"We ought not forget there is something vital and useful in the curious, if imperfect youth—something that shall not be stifled," the *Federalist* editors wrote.

Neil Gorsuch did not lose his sense of humor while at Columbia. Alongside his graduation picture he added a joke borrowed from Nixon's secretary of state Henry Kissinger, "The illegal we do immediately, the unconstitutional takes a little longer."

NEXT CAME HARVARD LAW School, to which Gorsuch had won a Truman Scholarship, a thirty-thousand-dollar grant from a program created by Congress in 1975. "The Truman Scholarship," says its website, "is a highly competitive, merit-based award offered to U.S. citizens and U.S. nationals from Pacific Islands who want to go to graduate school in preparation for a career in public service. Truman Scholars participate in leadership development programs and have special opportunities for internships and employment with the Federal government."

In 1975, the year the Truman Scholarships program was founded, Madeleine K. Albright said, "I can easily see tomorrow's Cabinet members, elected representatives, nonprofit directors—even presidents."

The former secretary of state was closer to an accurate prediction than she could have realized, for during Neil Gorsuch's three years at Harvard Law, a young man who also graduated from Columbia University *did* become president of the United States. His name is Barack Hussein Obama.

While the future president and the future Supreme Court justice attended Harvard at the same time, 1988–1991, Barack Obama had preceded Gorsuch at Columbia by five years. In 1979, Obama had moved to Los Angeles to attend Occidental College, and then transferred to Columbia as a junior. At Columbia, both Obama and Gorsuch majored in political science, but the future president added a specialty in international relations and another in English literature.

Shortly after Gorsuch was nominated, a lengthy article that appeared in the British publication *The Guardian* pointed up the sharp differences between the two high achievers, the liberal Obama and the conservative Gorsuch. "The campus was a place that was politically divided at the time and there was a lot of sometimes uncivil discussion about jurisprudence and other issues. Barack Obama and Neil Gorsuch were obviously on different sides of those issues," Bradford A. Berenson, a Boston-based corporate litigator who was one of Harvard Law's class of 1991 alongside the former president and the new Supreme Court nominee, told *The Guardian*.

Even though a typical Harvard Law class is a sea of five-hundred-plus ambitious, scholarly faces, Berenson said both Obama and Gorsuch stood out—for some contrasting but also similar reasons.

"They were both well-liked across the ideological spectrum and they were not obnoxious. I enjoyed being around them. Both were reserved, genial and respectful, but with a sense of humor. And they were both conspicuous talents at the time, in terms of legal intellect, but it was very clear then that Barack was a philosophical liberal and Neil was a conservative, much more straight-laced, a straight arrow," he said.

According to *The Guardian*, Harvard Law professor Laurence Tribe called Gorsuch "'a very, very bright judge'" who, he also recalled from his university days, was not just learned but "'very personable.'" But he knew Obama better, because the future president had been his research assistant.

Professor Tribe, also known as Larry, is a legal celebrity in his own right, having argued thirty-six cases before the U.S. Supreme Court. He has taught constitutional law at "the Law School" since 1968. Supreme Court Associate Justice Elena Kagan was one of his students.

The Guardian reported, "He recalls the young man who became the first black editor of the *Harvard Law Review* and then America's first black president as 'an incandescent intellectual, who was much more articulate than almost any student I have had in over 40 years.'" Obama drew attention as one of just a handful of minority students, of course, but Tribe said he was such a distinctive character and intellectual luminary that he would have stood out at Harvard regardless of skin color."

Upon leaving Harvard, Obama and Gorsuch took divergent paths. Obama went back to the South Side of Chicago to do community organizing, and the conventional Gorsuch went off to clerk on the Washington, D.C., circuit and then for Supreme Court justices Byron White and Anthony Kennedy.

According to *The Guardian*, "Gorsuch also won a scholarship to Oxford University in 1992 and began his PhD, in a formative trip where he met his British wife and further crystallized his conservative views. In later years, as a rising judge, Gorsuch would go to Tribe for suggestions for bright and independent-minded star students from the law school who would make good clerks for him. 'The people I can think of that I have recommended in the last 10 years or so have enjoyed working for him a great deal and liked him—and some of them were even liberal,' Tribe said."

Classmate Keith Boykin knew and respected both men, but, "as a budding progressive activist in the Black Students Association," has stronger recollections of the liberal Obama. "But what Boykin does recall about Gorsuch is that, while 'some conservatives there were very outspoken in a negative way to me, he was not one of them. It was a tense atmosphere on campus, a polarized environment, there were big issues being fought over, like lack of diversity in the faculty and the new dean at the time [Robert Clark] was very conservative and pro-business,'" Boykin said. *The Guardian* concluded, "So Gorsuch was not amongst the loud anti-liberal provocateurs, but he was unmistakably, staunchly conservative."

Another Harvard Law professor, Charles Fried, who had taught Obama, knew both men. As the faculty advisor of the Federalist Society at the university, he knew Gorsuch as a prominent member. "The Federalists later morphed to include lawyers and judges and such but it was a Harvard Law thing at the time with a charter declaring itself conservative, libertarian and, specifically, moderate—it was everybody but the left, basically. . . . Gorsuch has been nicknamed Antonin Scalia 2.0 as a supposed reflection of his vivid style and staunch conservatism."

Professor Fried noticed that not only were Gorsuch and Obama often linked in media accounts as their respective careers progressed, but so were Neil Gorsuch and Antonin Scalia. Professor Fried commented that both of the jurists wrote well, but then added, "[There] is not a sarcastic or aggressive remark from Gorsuch." Fried also pointed out that the two men are of opposite opinions on the so-called Chevron deference, "which can easily come into play in the administration of immigration, health, or environmental laws, for example. Scalia firmly believed federal government agencies have the overriding power to interpret statutes and the courts should 'greatly defer' to that, he said. 'Gorsuch thinks that's wrong. And that is ominous,'" said Fried.

Charles Fried also touched on the big open question: Would Neil Gorsuch vote to overturn *Roe* v. *Wade*? (One of the main reasons the question is open is that in his ten years as an appellate judge, Gorsuch did not rule on any cases that were directly related to the landmark decision that gave American women control over their own bodies.)

The same *Guardian* article quoted Professor Fried as saying, "I would suspect [Gorsuch] would join opponents [of *Roe* v. *Wade*] that have chipped away at the edges of the abortion right. Maybe it will be a case of 'you have the right but you may not be able to get [a termination] anywhere' because of all the regulatory hurdles," said Fried. "Having said that, Texas tried that and the Supreme Court reversed it," he added.

★

THE LEGAL CONCEPTS OF originalism and textualism in regard to interpreting the Constitution were frequently mentioned in the Gorsuch confirmation hearings. Briefly, originalists believe that the words of the Constitution *at the time it was adopted* should govern its application and interpretation today. Those opposed to originalism believe that questions are to be answered by using all available knowledge of both the past and present, including especially scientific knowledge that was not known or believed at the time the Constitution was written.

Textualism, often called a "close cousin" of originalism, is commonly defined as a belief that a law should be interpreted based on the plain meaning of its terms—and not on the *intent* of the legislators who passed it.

The late Justice Scalia is often called both an originalist and a textualist, but often stated that he was an originalist. Justice Gorsuch is also considered, both by himself and by others, an originalist, but not as doctrinaire as Scalia. At the time of the Gorsuch hearings, Robert Barnes, the legal reporter for the *Washington Post*, provided a helpful explanation of these often misused terms:

> Like the man whose seat he'd assume, the late Justice Antonin Scalia, Gorsuch is a proponent of originalism—meaning that judges should attempt to interpret the words of the Constitution as they were understood at the time they were written— and a textualist who considers only the words of the law being reviewed, not legislators' intent or the consequences of the decision.
>
> Critics say that those neutral considerations inevitably lead Gorsuch to conservative outcomes, a criticism that was also leveled at Scalia.

The Center for the Study of Constitutional Originalism at the University of San Diego School of Law defines it as "the view that the Constitution should be interpreted in accordance with its original meaning—that is, the meaning it had at the time of its enactment."

But I think University of Chicago law professor William Baude, an originalist scholar and former clerk for Supreme Court Chief Justice John Roberts, perhaps has the pithiest definition. "Baude defines it as 'the view that law laid down by the framers in the Constitution remains binding until we legally change it, such as through the amendment process.'

"'Or differently,' he said, 'that the words in the Constitution have the same meaning over time, even if modern circumstances change, and *even if we wish the words meant something else.*' (Emphasis added by me.)"

DURING HIS LAST TWO years of law school, a period marked by sit-ins outside the dean's office and inside the library and signs reading "Diversity Now" and "Homogeneity Feeds Hatred," Neil Gorsuch belonged to the Lincoln's Inn Society, a social club, and lived in its handsome Victorian home located off campus.

According to the *Boston Globe*, at one point, after neighbors complained that its loud parties resulted in leftover trash and parking problems, "He and other members of the Lincoln's Inn Society devised a 'management plan' to curb the rowdy behavior, while arguing the whole kerfuffle was overblown."

"'There are only six to eight parties a year,' Gorsuch assured the student newspaper, the *Harvard Law Review*, in November 1990. 'The Inn is more of a place to hang out.'"

Difficult as it may be to imagine the (mostly) somber and serious Neil Gorsuch of the televised nomination hearings "hanging out," on those rare moments when he took time from the book work, Gorsuch could be found shooting pool or lifting weights. According to the *Globe* story, "Twenty-six years later, classmates still describe Gorsuch . . . as more congenial than confrontational, even as he stood out as a committed conservative on a campus full of ardent liberals."

"Neil was among a small and relatively close-knit group of political and judicial conservatives on what was otherwise a very liberal campus, but he was not a controversial or hard-edged member of that group," said Brad Berenson, also a member of the class of 1991, who told the *Globe*, "He was pretty well respected across the board and really more a reserved and scholarly type that got along with everybody quite well, in a really politically divisive time."

But Gorsuch had other concerns on his mind, classmates said. He and his friends supported the Gulf War and term limits in Congress. And if the talk turned toward the lack of diversity on the faculty, they wanted to see not only more minorities but also more conservatives.

"'The conversation I recall was: How can we have increased diversity of all perspectives?' said Ken Mehlman, a fellow member of the Lincoln's Inn Society who went on to become chairman of the Republican National Committee and George W. Bush's campaign manager in 2004.

"Adam Charnes, another law school friend, described Gorsuch as unfailingly polite and humble in a class of sharp-elbowed overachievers. 'He was generally conservative, but certainly not a political firebrand of any sort,' Charnes said. 'He seemed to project sort of a western, laid-back image.' . . . But friends said Gorsuch was not the one blasting music at all hours. 'Neil was not any sort of a wild man on campus or in the years thereafter,' said Berenson, who served in Bush's White House. 'He's a straight, temperate guy.'"

"Bob Kroll, a fellow member of the Lincoln's Inn Society, described Gorsuch as less irascible than his classmates and more low-key—like that other famous member of the class of 1991. 'He had such a thoughtful manner, and he would weigh the issues in a way I found so insightful and so impressive,' Kroll said. 'I kind of felt that way about Barack Obama, too.'"

★

IN HIS NOMINATION ANNOUNCEMENT, President Trump said Gorsuch had worked at the Harvard Prison Legal Assistance Project and Harvard Defenders Program. In the next month, opponents of the nomination, people and publications alike, searched for anything to disqualify or discredit Neil Gorsuch, and his law school pro bono work became the subject of one of these attempts.

"There's something weird about Neil Gorsuch's history at Harvard," proclaimed an article in the *Boston Daily* (an offshoot of the *Boston Globe*) which credited the *Wall Street Journal*. "One big chunk of it—a part that makes him seem like a really nice guy—isn't adding up." The story said, "While he was a law student, he claims to have volunteered his legal expertise to help the less fortunate via the Harvard Prison Legal Assistance Project and Harvard Defenders. But the problem is, almost no one remembers him doing so."

But after that, the story dropped from sight. In the end, it turned out to be, to borrow the word used to describe the incident regarding loud parties at the Lincoln's Inn, a "kerfuffle."

A month later, a group of Gorsuch's law school classmates, of both political bents, signed a letter endorsing his nomination. It read, in part: "We attended law school with Judge Neil Gorsuch—a man we've known for more than a quarter century—and we unanimously believe Neil possesses the exemplary character, outstanding intellect, steady temperament, humility and open-mindedness to be an excellent addition to the United States Supreme Court. . . .

"Judge Neil Gorsuch," it continued, "is a person for all seasons. For Republicans, Neil personifies a disinterested philosophy that respects judicial modesty combined with compassionate appreciation of the lives impacted by his decisions. For Democrats, he is a reasonable, qualified, intelligent person who will give each case fair and impartial consideration on its merits with sensitivity to our nation's history, values, aspirations and constitutional traditions. For all Americans, he is a person of integrity who respects the rule of law and will ensure that it applies equally to all."

One of the letter's signers was a well-known Democrat, Norm Eisen, former ambassador to the Czech Republic, who had also been special counsel for ethics in President Obama's White House.

On April 4, three days before Gorsuch was confirmed by the Senate, there was another charge that also implied dishonesty on the part of the nominee. *Politico*, a political website that in the past has been accused of having a Republican bias and then later just the opposite, had consistently opposed the Gorsuch nomination. Its story, headlined "Gorsuch's writings borrowed from other authors," charged that passages in Gorsuch's 2006 book (*The Future of Assisted Suicide and Euthanasia*) "read nearly verbatim to a 1984 article in the *Indiana Law Journal*." It also accused him of plagiarizing passages from a seventeen-year-old academic article, stating, "Gorsuch borrowed from the ideas, quotes and structures of scholarly and legal works without citing them."

According to the article and other commentators, Gorsuch had cited the original sources used by the authors of the articles in question, but did not attribute them to the authors in whose works he had apparently found them.

The White House quickly quoted a set of plagiarism experts who said, in effect, no big deal, and the magazine countered with different experts who said the opposite. In the end, it appeared that, depending on which expert one chose to favor, while it could be considered plagiarism at one end of the definitional spectrum and just sloppy writing at the other, the issue did not appear to reveal a major flaw in the judge's character, especially in light of the very great amount of writing Gorsuch had done from 2006 to 2017 (during his confirmation hearings he told the committee that he had written or joined over six million words just as a federal judge).

In the end, like the issue of his pro bono work at Harvard Law School, the charge soon faded from prominence. To borrow a journalistic phrase, "The story did not have legs."

BASED ON THEIR PERFORMANCE while classmates at Harvard Law, both Barack Obama and Neil Gorsuch, the two undisputed stars of the class of 1991, had offers to clerk for prestigious judges on the federal level. But only one of them accepted.

Barack Obama decided to go home to Chicago and get involved in community service as an organizer. But when he told his girlfriend (Michelle Robinson, also Harvard Law, class of 1988, and later his wife), she was not pleased with his decision. She knew he was in the running for a clerkship with a former congressman from Illinois, Abner ("Abe") Mikva, the chief judge of the D.C. Circuit, a court—and a judge—famous for supplying clerks to the U.S. Supreme Court. Then and now, a clerk from the D.C. Circuit was all but guaranteed to be a Supreme Court clerk, after which the sky of the legal profession was the limit.

As Staci Zaretsky wrote in the legal blog *Above the Law*, Barack told Michelle, "If you're going to make change, you're not going to do it as a Supreme Court clerk," or words to that effect. Thereafter in the 1990s, Obama was known in certain legal circles as "the one who got away." Zaretsky added, "Prior to Judge Mikva's retirement, 24 of his clerks went on to become Supreme Court clerks, and Obama later awarded him with the Presidential Medal of Freedom."

IN 1991, AS THE rest of his Harvard Law graduating class rushed off to begin their life's work, most to join major law firms, and fewer to clerk for judges, Gorsuch was in the latter group. He applied for a position as a Supreme Court clerk. He was hired by his fellow Coloradoan Byron White.

When White retired in June, Gorsuch left for Oxford University, to which he had won a prestigious Marshall Scholarship, named for former secretary of state George C. Marshall. He would study for a PhD in law.

According to the Marshall program's current website, "Up to forty Scholars are selected each year to study at graduate level at an UK institution in any field of study. As future leaders, with a lasting understanding of British society, Marshall Scholars strengthen the enduring relationship between the British and American peoples, their governments and their institutions. Marshall Scholars are talented, independent and wide-ranging, and their time as Scholars enhances their intellectual and personal growth. Their direct engagement with Britain through its best academic programmes contributes to their ultimate personal success."

PhD candidates at Oxford take few classes; the bulk of their work is in independent reading followed by tutorial sessions with their major thesis advisor. In Gorsuch's case that was John Finnis, an Australia-born legal scholar and philosopher who specializes in the philosophy of law. Finnis is known for his strong belief in the doctrine of natural law, which holds that in addition to man-made laws there's a body of laws that stems from man's basic nature and that can be discovered by the use of reason. A 1962 convert to Catholicism, Dr. Finnis has been teaching at the University of Notre Dame since 1995.

"Oxford has probably the best philosophy program in the world, and Finnis happens to be one of the giants," said Leonard Leo, an adviser to Mr. Trump. Judge Gorsuch's work there "is a pretty significant distinction," he added.

Some of John Finnis's views are very controversial. For example, in defending his long-held position against same-sex marriage and same-sex coupling, he once compared them to bestiality.

During the confirmation hearings Senator Dick Durbin (D-IL) asked if Dr. Finnis's beliefs had influenced Gorsuch's judicial philosophy. The senator was so persistent in this line of questioning that for the first time in the hearings, the nominee's façade of calm patience seemed to crack a bit.

"During his Senate confirmation hearing for a Supreme Court seat," reported Time, "the Colorado judge appeared frustrated when pressed by Democratic Sen. Dick Durbin on the views of his dissertation advisor. The Illinois senator noted that Oxford law professor John Finnis once wrote that European countries were facing 'cultural decay from reverse colonization' caused by immigration, comparing the comment to a recent controversial tweet by Iowa Rep. Steve King.

"'I'm not here,' Gorsuch snapped back, 'to answer for Mr. King or for Professor Finnis. I've had a lot of professors . . . and I didn't agree with everything they said.'"

Durbin wasn't done. He countered by saying, "This is a man who apparently had an impact on your life, certainly your academic life. And I'm trying to figure out where we can parse his views from your views."

Gorsuch wasn't buying: "I think," he said ("growing visibly agitated," according to *Time*), "the best evidence is what I've written. I've written or joined over 6 million words as a federal appellate judge. I've written a couple of books. I've been a lawyer and a judge for 25 or 30 years. That's my record, and I guess I'd ask you, respectfully, to look at my credentials and my record."

AS HIS DISSERTATION SUBJECT, Neil Gorsuch had chosen assisted suicide, a topic much in the news at that time because of the ongoing notoriety surrounding Dr. Jacob "Jack" Kevorkian, the famous (some said infamous) proponent and practitioner of physician-assisted suicide, a practice that Gorsuch had long enjoyed debating with classmates and friends. It was also a topic dear to the heart of John Finnis. Like his advisor, Gorsuch opposed the practice. While Gorsuch did not agree with his former teacher on all issues, on this one they were definitely in sync.

After graduating from Oxford with his PhD, Gorsuch, with a contract in hand from Princeton University Press, turned his dissertation into a book. *The Future of Assisted Suicide and Euthanasia* was published in 2006, the same year he was named to the federal bench. According to the publisher, "After assessing the strengths and weaknesses of arguments for assisted suicide and euthanasia, Gorsuch builds a nuanced, novel, and powerful moral and legal argument against legalization, one based on a principle that, surprisingly, has largely been overlooked in the debate—the idea that human life is intrinsically valuable and that intentional killing is always wrong. At the same time, the argument Gorsuch develops leaves wide latitude for individual patient autonomy and the refusal of unwanted medical treatment and life-sustaining care, permitting intervention only in cases where an intention to kill is present."

The phrase "that human life is intrinsically valuable and that intentional killing is always wrong," which is Gorsuch's own, was cited by both pro- and con-Gorsuch camps as proof that if *Roe* v. *Wade*, the landmark case that legalized abortion, were to come before the Supreme Court again, Gorsuch would vote to overturn it. But at the time of his confirmation hearings for the Supreme Court, no one made that claim.

Writing about the book in 2017, former *SCOTUSblog* editor Amy Howe says, in part, that in the book Gorsuch devoted a whole chapter to analyzing the two major abortion cases other than *Roe* v. *Wade* (*Planned Parenthood* v. *Casey* and *Cruzan* v. *Director, Missouri Department of Health*), and concluded that they did not support a right to assisted suicide or euthanasia.

> Gorsuch devotes an entire chapter to an analysis of *Planned Parenthood v. Casey*, the Supreme Court's 1992 decision reaffirming a woman's right to an abortion, and *Cruzan v. Director, Missouri Department of Health*, the court's 1990 decision upholding the state's refusal to allow the parents of a woman in a "persistent vegetative state" to terminate treatment on her behalf. The question for Gorsuch is whether the two cases

support an interest in autonomy, protected by the Constitution, that could in turn support a right to assisted suicide and euthanasia. In his view, they do not.

Howe writes that in a footnote "Gorsuch stresses that his analysis in his book is limited to assisted suicide and euthanasia; he has no intent 'to engage the abortion debate.' But he doesn't stop at that. Instead, he acknowledges that 'abortion would be ruled out by the inviolability-of-life principle I intend to set forth *if*, but only *if*, a fetus is considered a human life.' Gorsuch then seems to pull back again, reminding his readers that in *Roe* the Supreme Court 'unequivocally held that a fetus is not a "person" for purposes of constitutional law'—suggesting, perhaps, that the issue has already been taken off the table."

Thus it appears that, when Gorsuch was confirmed, his statements in *The Future of Assisted Suicide and Euthanasia*, provocative as they may seem, do not rise to the level of accurate predictions as to his views on abortion. They are not, as a lawyer would say, *dispositive*.

Earning his advanced degree from Oxford put Neil Gorsuch in special company. Only two other justices had the same degree—John Marshall Harlan II and David Souter. (Justice Harlan, a conservative member of the Warren Court who served from 1955 to 1971, is not to be confused with his more famous grandfather John Marshall Harlan, 1877–1911.) Gorsuch's hero Byron White also attended Oxford, but did not receive a degree because he left in 1942 to join the navy as America's participation in World War II began in earnest. Gorsuch's Supreme Court colleague Stephen Breyer also has an Oxford degree, but his is a Bachelor of Arts, which he earned from Magdalen College in 1964.

Chapter Three

CLERKING

Upon his return to America, Gorsuch went to work as a clerk to Anthony Kennedy, who would become yet another important mentor. It was a pivotal year. As the *New York Times* reported on March 3, 2017, "Then 25 and fresh off a year at Oxford, Judge Gorsuch had been hired by Justice Byron R. White for the most coveted apprenticeship in American law—a Supreme Court clerkship. But because Justice White had retired, Judge Gorsuch was also assigned, by happenstance, to Justice Kennedy, the longtime center of power at the Supreme Court.

"His year as a clerk, beginning in the summer of 1993, gave Judge Gorsuch a privileged look at the Court's workings and a crash course in its unrelenting caseload and internal politics. As Judge Brett M. Kavanaugh of the United States Court of Appeals for the District of Columbia Circuit, and a fellow law clerk to Justice Kennedy that year who is on President Trump's short list should another Supreme Court vacancy occur, observed, 'We were in the middle of everything.' [In] the aftermath of a bruising term [and the] fallout of a divisive abortion case, *Planned Parenthood* v. *Casey*, had left the justices eager to produce a quieter one in its wake."

"'Look, there are a hundred people a year that could do the job adequately,'" Justice White once said, according to his biographer, Dennis J. Hutchinson. "I might as well have someone who's interesting,

and that doesn't mean the ones the fancy law professors recommend.'"
That Justice White was partial to candidates from his home state, Colorado, and to those who had spent time at Oxford, where the justice had been a Rhodes Scholar, most likely helped Gorsuch's application stand out, said two law clerks who worked for Justice White, David D. Meyer and John C. P. Goldberg. 'Justice White probably would have seen echoes of himself in a way in Neil,' said Mr. Meyer, who is now the dean of Tulane University Law School. Todd C. Peppers, who teaches at Roanoke College and has written extensively about Supreme Court law clerks, said Gorsuch's academic credentials might have glittered just a little less brightly than those of some of the clerks hired by active justices."

As Adam Liptak and Nicholas Fandos wrote in the *New York Times:*

Even clerks who worked for a single justice remembered a merciless workload. "It was the definition of a 24/7 job," said Landis C. Best, who worked for Chief Justice William H. Rehnquist and is now a partner at Cahill Gordon & Reindel in New York. Judge Gorsuch cut an impressive, if not particularly ideological, figure. Surrounded by a class of elite law graduates that included a handful of future federal judges and acclaimed academics, his "quiet intelligence" was notable, said Louis Feldman, who clerked for Justice Scalia that year. . . .

Mostly, Judge Gorsuch was affable and unflappable. He was not, by several former colleagues' accounts, a member of the regular pickup basketball games in the Supreme Court's fifth-floor gym, known around the building as the "highest court in the land." But he was a regular at clerk social events and occasional lunches hosted by each of the justices.

"He seemed very calm, measured, thoughtful, polite, gentlemanly—very much like what one notices about him now," said Eugene Volokh, an O'Connor clerk who teaches at the University of California, Los Angeles. According to Judge Kavanaugh, "He fit into the place very easily. He's just an easy guy to get along with. He doesn't have sharp elbows."

"We had a wide range of views, but we all really got along well," Judge Kavanaugh said of the five clerks who, said the *New York Times*, were chosen in part to represent the whole political spectrum.

When in 2006 Judge Gorsuch joined the United States Court of Appeals for the Tenth Circuit, Justice Kennedy administered the oath to him in Denver and then explained the significance of the oath to the judge's two young daughters, Justice Kennedy said, "He's doing it to remind all of us that the first obligation any American has is to defend and protect the Constitution of the United States."

Neil Gorsuch's year of service to Stephen Breyer showed the young clerk how a true gentleman of the law went about his job. The instruction by example took.

EACH YEAR THE COURT receives thousands of petitions for certiorari, i.e., "cert petitions," in which the petitioners ask the Court to hear their case. Although the Court hears but a fraction of them in a single term, each petition is read—and read carefully—by a clerk whose justice takes part in what is called the cert pool.

White did not join the pool, but Kennedy did, and in the fall of 1993 Neil Gorsuch found himself reading a cert petition named *Martinez-Hidalgo* v. *United States*. This 1991 case involved the boarding of a twenty-six-foot flagless boat—meaning one without a name or identification numbers—whose crew said the boat was from Colombia. After obtaining a "statement of no objection" from the Colombian government, the Coast Guard searched the boat, discovering 282 kilos of cocaine. The crew was charged with possession and intent to distribute the drug and later convicted in federal court. One of the crew, Martinez-Hidalgo, challenged the conviction in a petition for cert to the U.S. Supreme Court. It fell to Neil Gorsuch to analyze the record of the case and write a memo that stated whether the petition should be either granted or denied.

In an eleven-page memo, he wrote, "It seems clear that the [due process] issue raised by this case has broad legal significance, questioning as it does the extraterritorial reach of both Congress and the Constitution. That said, it is not at all clear that the case has (at this point) much practical significance; [petitioner] points to no large, extant class of [defendants] for whom a decision here would make any real difference."

Gorsuch further advised that the legal dispute was "the faintest of splits" and that it "dissipates on examination." (Real splits on federal legal questions among the federal circuits are a key reason the Court grants review of a case.) Gorsuch felt that the petitioner's "briefing at the cert stage does not bode well for merits briefing," he wrote, meaning it didn't have much chance of moving forward and onto the Court's docket.

According to Eugene Volokh, law professor and frequent blogger on legal matters (and a longtime friend of Gorsuch), clerks' cert memos "have been used before as fodder in high court confirmation battles, most recently during the 2010 hearing for Elena Kagan. A few conservatives criticized Kagan for a cert memo she wrote to Justice Thurgood Marshall, for whom she clerked in the October 1987 term, regarding a school district's race-conscious high-school-attendance rezoning plan. Kagan, in her memo to Marshall, called the voluntary plan 'amazingly sensible' and urged him to vote to deny review of the case, which the court did.

"One conservative testified before the Senate Judiciary Committee that Kagan's stance would give administrators license to engage in 'racial engineering.' The charge didn't make much headway with the committee criteria," said Volokh.

"But" according to Mark Walsh, writing in *SCOTUSblog*, "Gorsuch's cert pool memos provide a window on one key part of his clerkship. Justice Harry Blackmun, who was in his last term in 1993–94, was a member of the cert pool, like Kennedy. Blackmun preserved almost everything from his years of judicial service in his files, including clerk memos from the cert pool. Blackmun's papers were first made publicly available at the Library of Congress in 2004. Clerk memos tend to be somewhat formulaic and cautious. . . . They perhaps reveal little about how a former law clerk might approach issues he might confront later in life as a Supreme Court justice.

"In another case, Gorsuch explored for ten pages an Arizona prison inmate's arguments that his mandatory 'hard labor' crafting novelty belt buckles in a prison-run program qualified him as an 'employee' under the Fair Labor Standards Act. A federal district court and the Ninth Circuit held otherwise.

"Gorsuch concluded that the inmate's petition did not present a circuit split, as asserted, between the Ninth Circuit and two other federal circuits that had ruled prisoners to be employees because they worked for non-prison entities. 'The [court of appeals] "split" is more apparent than real,' Gorsuch wrote. 'No [court of appeals] has held a prisoner working for the prison institution or in a prison-sponsored work program to be a FLSA employee. . . .

"'Now, perhaps if [the Ninth Circuit] were to go on in some future case to argue that a "state-structured program" includes working for McDonald's, a conflict with other circuit rulings would surely emerge.'"

Mark Walsh added, "Gorsuch's writing style in the memos is crisp and approachable, occasionally employing nice turns of phrase. In a petition stemming from a labor-organizing dispute at a North Carolina chicken-processing plant, Gorsuch discussed how the U.S. solicitor general had done 'an artful job' of distinguishing the case in question from a National Labor Relations Board decision known as Standard Products. 'This case and Standard Products may sit uneasily together, but they can be coaxed into getting along,' Gorsuch wrote."

Walsh had one minor complaint: "[Gorsuch] did have a penchant for using stodgy terms, such as 'amongst,' 'whilst,' and 'unbeknownst.' One of Justice Blackmun's clerks, in marking up a memo from Gorsuch, circled one of his uses of 'whilst' in an apparent equivalent of an eye roll."

The Blackmun papers referred to above contain fifty cert memos written by Gorsuch, and in almost all of them he recommended denying review. In the case of a prisoner who was seeking relief as a pauper (*in forma pauperis*, in Courtspeak), he wrote: "Habeas [petitioner] seeks error correction" to overturn his murder and robbery conviction. "All questions presented are factbound; nothing remotely certworthy lurking here. Deny."

In the case of a high school student who was involved in a carjacking and got sentenced to twelve years, Gorsuch was sympathetic, writing that the boy was the "school's star football athlete and had the chance to attend college on scholarship," and that "several teachers [had] submitted letters attesting to [petitioner's] character."

Yet, sympathy aside, Gorsuch called the defendant's claim of ineffective assistance of counsel "enormously fact-laden . . . implicating no splits, and raising no important question of law. . . . It seems to me that the sentence imposed here was horribly harsh; but to intervene would constitute error-correction alone." (This Gorsuch opinion, written as a twenty-six-year-old law clerk, might be read as foreshadowing his Tenth Circuit ruling, years later, in the TransAm trucker case, in which he was faulted for what some lawyers felt was an over-reliance on the law as written, in contrast to a more lenient approach that might have better suited the petitioner.)

In the case of an inmate in Tennessee who claimed he was assaulted with a broomstick by another inmate and had unsuccessfully sued two jail employees for not preventing the attack, Gorsuch called the cert petition "frivolous" and a "clear deny on the merits." He went further, suggesting that the justices might consider denying pauper status to the petitioner based on a Supreme Court rule that permits such denials when a petition is clearly frivolous.

But Gorsuch showed considerable sympathy for a petitioner who argued that the police had exceeded their authority when, following a routine traffic stop, she and a passenger were put into a police car while the police, with her consent, searched her car. During the women's in-the-car conversation, which was recorded without their knowledge, they made what Gorsuch, in his memo, described as "several tape-recorded inculpatory statements." After the police found a large amount of cocaine in the car, the women were arrested.

The driver sought to suppress the recording, claiming the police had violated her "reasonable expectation of privacy in her conversation with her friend. Two lower courts rejected the argument."

"In a nine-page memo," wrote Walsh, "Gorsuch suggested the justices 'call for a response' from the respondent, a tactic used in potentially certworthy cases when a government agency has initially waived its right to respond.

"'As appalling as the police behavior here was,' he wrote, '. . . it does seem fairly clear that [petitioner] voluntarily consented to the search of her vehicle, thus perhaps invalidating what might otherwise have been an impermissible search. . . .' (The court denied the petition outright.)"

GORSUCH'S 1993–94 LAW CLERK class included other young lawyers who went on to careers of prominence, including former U.S. solicitor general Paul Clement (who clerked for Justice Antonin Scalia) and Judge Brett Kavanaugh (a Kennedy clerk) of the U.S. Court of Appeals for the District of Columbia Circuit, both of whom have been mentioned as potential Supreme Court picks for a Republican president. Other clerks in the 1993 term included Julius Genachowski (Justice David Souter), who served as chairman of the Federal Communications Commission under President Obama; James Ryan (Chief Justice Rehnquist), now the dean of the Harvard Graduate School of Education; and Allison Eid (Justice Clarence Thomas), now a member of the Colorado Supreme Court.

"You're feeling lucky to be around such top young lawyers from all over the country," Volokh told Walsh of *SCOTUSblog*.

WHILE THE GENERAL PUBLIC is aware that Supreme Court justices hire several law clerks for each new term of the Court, they have little idea of what the job entails. In early 1992, I found out by writing about some former clerks for *Washington Lawyer*, the magazine of the District of Columbia bar association ("Supreme Clerks," John Greenya, *Washington Lawyer*, May–June 1992), the year before Neil Gorsuch was a clerk on the Supreme Court.

The first former high court clerk I wrote about was Joseph Rauh, Jr., the renowned civil rights and labor lawyer: "It was my final year in law school, and I was walking down the hallway when my mentor and idol, Professor Felix Frankfurter, stopped me and said, 'Mr. Rauh, what are you doing next year?' I said, 'I have an offer from the largest Jewish law firm in Cincinnati.' And he said, 'Well, you write them and tell them you're not coming. I have something in mind.'"

That "something" turned out to be a clerkship on the United States Supreme Court for Justice Benjamin Cardozo. History had smiled on young Joe Rauh, who served as the last clerk to Justice Cardozo and the first to Associate Justice Felix Frankfurter. Joe Rauh has been a watcher of the Supreme Court—and Supreme Court clerks—ever since, more than fifty-five years.

He relates, with characteristic self-effacement, how he became a lawyer in a sense by default, and a Supreme Court clerk almost by happenstance. When he graduated from Harvard in 1932, there were no jobs to be had, and seeing as an older brother had preceded him into the family business, he went to law school. In his third year he finally got to take a course from a man he already revered, Felix Frankfurter.

"He took a shine to me, and I, naturally, was mesmerized by him. He would leave every week and go down and spend a couple of days at the White House helping to run the New Deal. It was just exciting to be near him.

"I took his seminar in federal jurisdiction, a course in which we read the Supreme Court advance sheets, and then discussed the opinions—this was the anti–New Deal court—and, as I said, he took a shine to me. He chose [all] the Brandeis law clerks, and the Cardozo law clerks every third time.

"The year I got out of law school, 1935, Cardozo had the second year of a clerk from Yale, so Frankfurter had me work for Ben Cohen and Tom Corcoran [two of the most important of FDR's brain trust of New Deal lawyers] from '35 to '36, and then appointed me in 1936, and I remained until Cardozo died in '38.

"The Supreme Court clerk of today [1992] would hardly recognize the job." As Rauh puts it, "The relationship in those days, when there was one clerk, while now there are four [to each justice], was totally different. I was Justice Cardozo's *son* for two years. It had nothing to do with whether I was a good lawyer or a bad lawyer, it was that his life so totally revolved around the Court that he needed a prop. He didn't need me for any legal help—God knows he was self-sufficient—but he needed someone for just companionship. It was a beautiful relationship.

"Cardozo, you have to realize, was by this time totally lonesome. His father was a Tweed Ring judge in New York City who had to resign in disgrace, and the story always was that Cardozo had devoted his life to making the name honorable again. It was common knowledge, but I don't know if it was true or not because I never got close enough to him to talk to him about it."

In those days the judges' conference was held on Saturday afternoon, and at 7:00 p.m. the chief justice, Charles Evans Hughes, would make the writing assignments. Rauh still has a vivid memory of the first conference during his time as a clerk.

"I missed the first one! I had gone home. It was Saturday afternoon and we worked six days, and I'd gone home mid-afternoon. So when I walked in Monday morning, there was something he said that indicated he would have been glad to have had me there. . . . And so I never missed another one. But when I walked in Monday morning he had a draft of the opinion. Cardozo's apartment at 2101 Connecticut Avenue [still a very distinguished Northwest Washington address] had long, long hallways, and they were all lined with bookcases filled with the Supreme Court, federal, and New York opinions. He knew those very well. What he would often say to me was, 'Mr. Rauh, I have put in the Supreme Court, the federal, and the relevant New York cases. Would you get some from New Mexico or someplace out there so I don't look so parochial?'"

At one point Cardozo told his law clerk that he thought he had once read, somewhere, that there had been head taxes in the Colonies. He asked him to check it out. "That was the only hard job I ever had. I went to the congressional law library and I asked somebody in a position of knowledge what to do, and he took me into the dustiest room I'd ever seen, I don't think anybody had been in it for years. It had all the statutes of all the Colonies. The dust was as thick as could be, and I looked like a mine worker when I got out of the place. But Cardozo had been absolutely right. I got the statutes and the citations, and he was gleeful!"

Rauh pauses and laughs. "But then, whatever you did, he praised it—you just couldn't do anything wrong—he was just the most generous, warm man."

"IF YOU ASKED, 'DID you ever write an opinion?' the answer to that would be, 'Hell, no.' If I got a sentence or three words in an opinion, I thought I'd done a day's work. He wrote them all, and he wrote them between Saturday night and Monday morning."

When Rauh was a clerk the pay was, as he puts it, "the munificent sum of $2,600 a year." In 1992 when this article was written, Rauh said, "While the workload is staggering, the clerks (who make $38,861 a year) do get together for the occasional 'happy hour.'"

In Rauh's day there was little of that collegiality. "The Supreme Court was in a temporary turmoil, as President Roosevelt tried to thwart the high-court foes of his New Deal legislation by adding up to six more justices—one for every justice who refused to retire at age 70. I probably had the best seat in America for the court-packing plan."

In 1938, following Cardozo's death from heart problems, FDR appointed Felix Frankfurter to the Supreme Court. After years of choosing clerks for others, Frankfurter now had to choose one for himself. As his first law clerk, he chose his former student Joe Rauh.

"It was midyear, and it wasn't easy to find the right clerk," says Rauh, "and I told Ben Cohen to tell the justice—as it would have been arrogant to tell him myself—that if he really wanted someone to take it for the interim period, why, I would be glad to. It was some convenience to him to have somebody who knew his way around the Court.

"Eventually, there were two, three, four clerks for each justice, and pretty soon the thing became different. But while I was there, there was still only one clerk."

The next former Supreme Court clerk I interviewed for my 1992 article was Karen Hastie Williams, who has a lot of firsts on her resume. One of the most intriguing items is that she was a clerk for her own godfather, who happened to be Thurgood Marshall.

"I was born right here in Washington, D.C. I spent my first years here, and then went down to the Virgin Islands when my father became governor of the Virgin Islands, and from there to Philadelphia when he was appointed to the Third Circuit. I went to college in Maine, Bates College, then worked my way back down the East Coast, spending a year in Boston in graduate school at Tufts' Fletcher School of Law and Diplomacy, and decided I'd see what the real world looked like and worked for two years in New York at Mobil Oil Corporation. Next I came down to Washington and then decided I would stop fighting it and go to law school, and went to Catholic University Law School here, and then went from CU to clerk first for Judge [Spottswood] Robinson on the District of Columbia Circuit Court and then for Justice [Thurgood] Marshall," who happened to be her godfather. In 1992 she was a partner with the office of Crowell & Moring.

Williams recalls that when Judge Robinson made her one of his clerks, he told her, "'Now if you don't mess up, I can recommend you to Thurgood,' and I said, 'Oh God, he'd never hire me; I know him too well.' So when TM called me and said, 'Well? Are you going to come and work for me, or am I going to have to go out and find another law clerk?' I said, 'If you think you can stand having me work for you.' And he laughed and said, 'I'm tough!'

"I think everyone thought, 'You know him so well, you're his goddaughter, he's going to be easy on you.' And I said, 'No, I don't think so. I know him well enough to know that he's going to be as rough on me as he is on everyone else. He wants to toughen me up, and I want to do the best possible job I can for him.'"

She was right. "TM" was an equal-roughness employer. "It was very different clerking for him and being in that relationship, different than the family relationship we'd had before. He was very demanding. He wants his clerks to really push the edge of the envelope, if you will, in terms of applying precedents, of looking for new ways to attack problems, and I think the real legacy of the Marshall era was his humanizing of the law."

Williams, who calls her Supreme Court clerkship simply "a credential I prize," says of Justice Marshall, "He imbued his clerks with the sense of looking at the way issues impact people. Whether it was a state regulatory issue or a tax issue or a civil rights issue, it was the human impact involved. And I think that is the legacy of the decisions he wrote. I think he viewed his dissents as writing for history. . . . There was a major shift on the court from the Warren years through the Rehnquist-Scalia years when it was clear that he would not be writing for the majority; that never slowed him down, in terms of the intellectual rigor and vigor that he wanted his clerks in the first instance, and himself in the second, to put into the opinions. He felt very strongly about the leadership potential of the Supreme Court."

For Williams, the main point was her professional association with "TM." "The thrill of the clerkship," she says, "was working for someone who had devoted his whole life to the law."

ANOTHER FORMER SUPREME COURT clerk interviewed for my *Washington Lawyer* article, which was published one year before Neil Gorsuch worked as a Supreme Court clerk, was thirty-five-year-old Brian Martin, who clerked for Chief Justice Warren Burger in 1984–85.

At the time I interviewed him, Martin was of counsel to Barnes and Thornberg, an Indianapolis firm with a Washington, D.C., office. But at the time of the interview, Brian Martin did not work in either Indiana or the District of Columbia. Instead, he had carved out an ideal, and for him idyllic, situation: He lived and worked (mostly writing appellate briefs) on a sparsely populated island off the coast of Maine.

Martin said he didn't know of another firm that would have agreed to let him run his Washington-Indianapolis law practice from his home on Peaks Island, Maine, and he was most happy when Barnes and Thornburg did.

"I have an office in my home, and I have my own computer equipment and modem to call in to the firm's computer in Washington and in Indianapolis. In the morning I turn on the machine and check my messages; I have a fax machine with a separate line, and I have a secretary in Indianapolis. If you're in Indianapolis or Washington, all you have to do is hit three numbers on your phone, and it'll ring in Maine. In big firms now, you can be on a different floor, and not really know who's upstairs, right? So if someone wants to get in touch with me, it's just like I was on another floor. I've been doing this for a year and a half, and it's worked out wonderfully."

Martin said that contrary to what some people may think, a clerk's—or potential clerk's—politics rarely determine whether he or she gets the job. But what if the belief involved a social, legal, religious, or political issue such as abortion—would that change things?

"I don't think so. If you were talking to the justices, they would probably say, 'I have views on abortion, but my law clerk doesn't need to have views. I need to have someone I can trust who's smart and can keep secrets and that sort of thing.'

"A lot of the work," says Martin, ". . . is reviewing petitions for cert. At that time there were six justices who pooled law clerks, in the sense that one of the law clerks from those six justices would review the cert petition, the brief in opposition, and write a memorandum describing the case, the parties' arguments, and a section of legal analysis, which may also include a discussion of whether the issue's important."

As with any job, there were rituals, and they varied according to the justice involved. Martin says that while Justice Harry Blackmun had breakfast with his clerks almost every day, the Burger clerks had a quite different ritual. "On Saturdays, the Chief tended to make our lunch. The chief justice has a small kitchen in his chambers. He might make soup, or bring leftovers from home. So, if I was not working, my co-clerks would call me and say, 'Brian, get in here, the Chief's making lunch.'"

After my article ran, Brian Martin contacted me to say that he'd received a good-humored note from the retired chief justice, who denied that he had ever brought in "leftovers" for his clerks to eat. Everything, he said, was freshly made and served for the first time.

Chapter Four

LOVE AND MARRIAGE

NEIL WENT TO OXFORD TO GET A PhD . . . AND
CAME BACK WITH A WIFE AND A HORSE.

—*Gorsuch friend David Jarden*

Reports of the initial meeting between Neil and Louise, his future wife, usually say it was on a blind date, but a few others
call it a meeting at a party. However, on March 18, 2017, Associated
Press reporters Nancy Benac and Mark Sherman told a somewhat
different story.

"It's poker night in a row house on Cranham Street, Oxford,
England," they wrote, "and Neil Gorsuch, studying for yet another
degree, is feeling down. His housemates decide that what Gorsuch
needs is a girlfriend. Accounts differ on whether it was a dare, goad-
ing, or a gentle prod, but Gorsuch phones a woman he'd clicked with
during a school dinner more than a year earlier—and she doesn't remember him. Awkward.

"That 1994 phone call may be one of the few times that
Gorsuch . . . didn't immediately stand out from the crowd. [None-
theless] Louise Burletson agreed to go out with him anyway, and
ultimately married [him]."

★

GORSUCH WAS BACK IN England to finish his dissertation, and, whatever the exact story was, he in fact met and dated an attractive brunette named Marie Louise Burletson, also an Oxford graduate (degrees in both history and philosophy). He was getting his PhD in law and she was in graduate school studying business. Neil soon learned that Louise shared his love for the outdoors, animals (she'd been a member of the Oxford equestrian team), and laughter, and the early dates turned into a romance.

In 1996, they were married in St. Nicholas's (Protestant) Church in Louise's hometown of Henley-on-Thames, which is about forty miles from London. One tourism website proclaimed it one of the most beautiful towns in England, noting that the *Times* of London voted the town "one of the best places to live in the English countryside."

Louise was born in 1968 (one year after Neil) to Prudence and Bryan Burletson. She was christened at Hurley Church, raised in the Church of England, and attended the Rupert House School in Henley, St. Mary's, Wantage, and the Abbey School in Reading.

As the AP story said, "Though Neil Gorsuch swept Louise away from the UK and far from her family—her parents and older brother, Richard, still live across the pond—her family immediately took a liking to her future husband. . . . For the Burletson family, Neil was welcomed from day one." Louise's father told the local paper that Neil was "always a loving and totally supporting boyfriend [who] rapidly became very popular with everyone he met.

"It also helped, her father noted, that Gorsuch 'has always been a great anglophile and a major fan of Winston Churchill.'

"In 1996, the family had moved to the United States and Louise settled into the life of a young wife and mother in the D.C. suburb of Vienna, Virginia. She missed the open countryside of her youth back in England, and when her husband was made a federal appellate court judge by President George W. Bush in 2006, she looked forward to living in Colorado. They settled in Boulder, a picturesque city 25 miles west of Denver at the base of the foothills of the Rocky Mountains, and she quickly readopted her outdoor life style."

In 2017, Louise Gorsuch's friend Katy Fassett told Fox News, "My favorite time spent with Louise is running in the open space with our five dogs while she recounts hilarious anecdotes that make seven miles feel more like two. . . . [S]he embraced the backcountry lifestyle in Colorado." The article continued: "The family raised horses, chickens and goats. . . . But her friends say that while she loves the backcountry, she can quickly adapt to the hustle-and-bustle of Washington, D.C."

"The wonderful thing about Louise," says Michael Trent, a longtime friend of Judge Gorsuch and who was best man at his wedding, "is that she can be just as comfortable looking beautiful at the White House or in her wellies, shoveling horse manure by the barn."

That Neil Gorsuch remains mindful of how much his British wife gave up for him was evidenced by the fact he planted a rose garden for her in Boulder so she could enjoy her favorite flower, and by this statement he made before the Judiciary Committee: "We started off in a place very different than this one, tiny apartment, little to show for it. And when Louise's mother first came to visit, she was concerned by the conditions, understandably. As I headed out the door to work, I'll never forget her whispering to her daughter in a voice I think intended to be just loud enough for me to hear: 'Are you sure he's really a lawyer?'"

THE READER IS CAUTIONED not to read too much into this fact, but in 1996, when Neil Gorsuch married Louise Burletson, his hair was still dark, as is clearly evident from the wedding pictures. In the less than two decades since the nuptials, in which he went from Supreme Court law clerk to attorney in private practice to public servant to federal appeals court judge, the original brown has given way, entirely, to a premature grayish white. His wife, on the other hand, despite leaving her homeland to raise two daughters in the United States, and, once in America, move from the East Coast to the West, still closely resembles her wedding photos.

The couple's first daughter, Emma, was born in Colorado in 1999, and their second, Belinda, whom they call "Bindy," two years later.

Fox News reporter Kristine Kotta, who profiled the couple for an April 20, 2017, story, wrote:

> The British native comes from a religious upbringing and holds degrees in both history and philosophy. She met her future husband while she was attending graduate school at Oxford. He was a law student there and they met on a blind date in 1995. . . . Toward the end of his remarks [in the Supreme Court confirmation hearings] that day, Gorsuch turned to his wife, who was behind him and said: "To my wife, Louise, and my daughters, Emma and Bindy, thank you for your perseverance and your patience, your courage and your love. I simply could not have attempted this without you."

One Gorsuch relative, Margaret Sampson Gorsuch, Neil's father's second wife, and since 2002, his widow, did speak to the press, but not the American press. On February 3, 2017, the *Daily Mail*, a British paper, ran a story entitled "Supreme Court Pick Neil Gorsuch's Family Breaks Silence," which began:

The stepmother of President Trump's Supreme Court pick toasted the news of his nomination with champagne and pizza, saying he will do a "wonderful" job. Margaret Gorsuch, 83, of Denver, Colorado, has known stepson Neil since he was a teenager, and was married to his lawyer father David until his death 15 years ago. Gorsuch's parents divorced in 1982 and his mother Anne also went on to remarry rancher Robert Burford. He died in 1993, and Anne passed away of cancer aged just 62 in 2004.

Margaret told DailyMail.com that she remains close to the 49-year-old and regularly sees the judge and his "lovely" British wife Marie Louise for lunch and at family gatherings.

Speaking about her stepson, she said: "He's brilliant, he's disciplined, he's handsome, he's witty—what else do you need to know? His wife is the most beautiful British woman, she's lovely. The whole family are very pleased with him." . . .

[Neil Gorsuch made an equally big hit with his new in-laws in England, Louise's] parents Bryan and Prudence Burletson. Louise's father . . . a retired property developer, declined to comment on his son-in-law's potential elevation. [But the] . . . family are close despite the distance they live from each other, and Gorsuch thanked his parents-in-law for their support in the foreword to his book on suicide and euthanasia.

★

THROUGHOUT HIS LIFE, IT has been noticed and remarked upon that Neil Gorsuch makes friends easily and, as his earliest report cards undoubtedly said, "plays well with others." "Who is Neil Gorsuch?" asked the Associated Press on March 18, 2017:

Among the answers: On his birthday, his family must watch a Western with him; he runs with his law clerks, instructs them in "the Zen of fly-fishing," and on the ski slopes, waits at the top to see which of them he'll have to help get up after a fall; knows the names of the security guards at the courthouse and asks about their families; and, says former clerk Joshua Goodbaum, is the kind of person "who talks about the law for fun."

But not everyone thought these traits qualified him to sit on the Supreme Court. Ilyse Hogue, president of NARAL Pro-Choice America, said, "I'm hearing he's a really nice guy. That's way too low a bar for a jurist on the highest court in the land."

QUITE NATURALLY, THE VIEW from inside the family circle is totally positive. His brother, J.J., a Denver marketing company executive, told the media that his big brother was "always on the brainy side," and that theirs was a typical western childhood, filled with family trips for outdoor recreation. The AP wrote that "even Gorsuch's childhood mischief tended toward the intellectual—he once read a book about gambling and put it to use by starting a basement casino for neighborhood kids."

Neil and J.J.'s sister, Stephanie, the youngest of the three Gorsuch children, is the director of money transfers for Western Union, where she has worked since 2011. Stephanie is equally supportive of her oldest sibling, but is seldom quoted in the media, preferring to keep her opinion private.

★

THROUGHOUT HIS LIFE, NEIL Gorsuch has displayed a facility for making—and keeping—friends. As the *Washington Post* reported in its long article on him shortly after the president named him as his Supreme Court nominee:

> Gorsuch has also established deep and enduring relationships
> with liberals he has known since his school days—in some
> cases the very targets of his pointed attacks. He has won
> endorsements from gay friends and hired law clerks from the
> opposite end of the political spectrum. He has argued that
> the court system shortchanges low-income people and called
> for making legal services cheaper and courts more accessible.
> Even the simple writing style of his opinions, which have
> won wide attention in legal circles, reflects his conviction that
> the law should be understandable to everyone, lest it favor
> only the wealthy and well educated.
>
> In his writings, he has denounced liberals for using court
> decisions to advance "their social agenda." But Gorsuch has
> also refused to be pigeonholed himself, saying, "People do
> unexpected things. Pigeonholes ignore gray areas in the law."

At the time of Neil Gorsuch's nomination to the high court, grade school friends such as Gina Carbone, Rob Tengler, and Jonathan Brody spoke to the media in glowing terms about their time with him, as did Michael Trent, Thad Ficarra, and Brian Cashman, classmates at Georgetown Prep. At both Columbia and Harvard, Gorsuch made friends who have remained his friends for decades, like law school classmate Phil Berg, now a friend for more than thirty years.

Shortly after Berg married his boyfriend, he received a note from Neil telling them that if they were ever in Colorado, his house would be their house.

According to the *Washington Post*, "Many of those who knew Gorsuch during his student days noted that he was as affable in person as he was fierce in his writings."

Berg said Gorsuch was constantly establishing such connections with others, regardless of their political philosophy: "He would have a real conversation with people from the top professors to waiters and waitresses at a restaurant. He sort of put himself in their shoes," he said. "He made you feel like you were the only person in the room when he was talking to you."

Classmates and acquaintances—from his time in college, law school, and Oxford—uniformly describe him in effusive terms.

"There are a whole lot of people at Harvard Law School who are interested in talking and want you to think that they're the most important person in the room," said Ken Mehlman, his Harvard housemate and a former chairman of the Republican National Committee. "But Neil was very curious about other people and learning what they had to say."

Mehlman, like Berg, would later come out to Gorsuch as gay and also recalled the sensitive way he took the news.

"I would be surprised if any of our classmates had an unkind word to say about him," said Norm Eisen, a Harvard Law classmate who later became a high-ranking official in Obama's administration.

No one who knew Neil Gorsuch in his student days would describe him as a hell-raiser or a rabble-rouser (though his writings while at Columbia were hardly mild). His first boss in private practice, Mark Hansen, once said of him that he "looked like he had never walked against a Don't Walk sign." But over the years, by dint of hard work and concentration, he has become a fierce advocate for the principles and ideas he considers important.

★

SHORTLY AFTER NEIL GORSUCH was nominated for a seat on the Supreme Court to replace the late Antonin Scalia, liberal commentators wondered if his avowed friendship with several gay people could mean that once on the Court he would also be friendly toward the rights of the LGBTQ community, but Mark Joseph Stern, who covers the law and LGBTQ issues for *Slate*, threw a columnful of cold water on the idea with his article entitled "Neil Gorsuch Has Gay Friends. Who Cares?" It began: "[T]he *New York Times* published a very strange story by Sheryl Gay Stolberg titled 'Gorsuch Not Easy to Pigeonhole on Gay Rights, Friends Say.' The article notes that Neil Gorsuch '. . . has gay friends and is not outwardly homophobic in his interactions with them. Indeed, Stolberg explains at length, Gorsuch is actually *friendly* with these gay friends, congratulating them on their marriages and inviting them to stay in his guest room. Even better, he lives in Boulder, Colorado—a liberal city!—and goes to a church that 'welcomes gay members.'

"'That leads some friends to wonder if his jurisprudence might be closer to that of Justice Anthony Kennedy,' Stolberg writes, 'who has carved out a name for himself as the court's conservative defender of gay rights.'"

Stern disagrees, writing, "This conflation of personal and jurisprudential views is misguided and befuddling. There is little reason to think that Gorsuch's friendships with gay people will affect his legal views one way or the other. And it is especially unwise, in the run-up to his confirmation battle, to pretend that Gorsuch's associations will somehow push him toward a more progressive stance on LGBTQ rights. . . .

"How can we uncover Gorsuch's genuine beliefs about LGBTQ rights before he is elevated to the bench? Michelangelo Signorile argues that senators must ask him about gay rights, and I certainly agree—but I doubt these queries will yield much useful information. Gorsuch is adept at concealing his beliefs. . . . Do not expect Gorsuch to show his cards when senators ask about gay equality."

Stern concludes: "I have no doubt that Gorsuch's gay former classmates and clerks genuinely see him as an LGBTQ ally. But the fact remains that these amicable associations tell us virtually nothing about his jurisprudence. A review of his past decisions, on the other hand, reveals a judge who is quite skeptical of LGBTQ claims and hesitant to insist that the government be made to respect LGBTQ people's dignity. These rulings and writings, while relatively scarce, tell us more about his legal convictions than any personal ties possibly could. And they do not give LGBTQ Americans much cause for optimism."

WHAT *DOES* GIVE GORSUCH supporters cause for optimism is their belief in his basic humanity and his gift for listening—sincerely and carefully—to opposing views and the people who hold them.

Chapter Five

THE PRACTICE OF LAW

In 1995, armed with a law degree from Harvard, a doctorate in philosophy of law from Oxford, and experience as a clerk for three federal judges (two of them associate justices of the U.S. Supreme Court), family man Neil Gorsuch was about to look for a regular job for the first time since he had been a summer associate while in law school. But the reverse happened. A job looked for him—and he took it. Many who knew him expected he would walk off with yet another prize, this one in the form of a higher-than-average starting salary with a high-profile, nationally known firm, but he surprised them by choosing a two-year-old start-up law firm in the nation's capital.

He chose the firm—Kellogg, Huber, Hansen, Todd, Evans & Fiegel—because it had decided to get proactive in the hiring of former Supreme Court clerks, those cream-of-the-crop young lawyers who were just finishing their clerkships and coming on the legal job market for the first time. In the usual course of Big Law business, they would be hired by the large, well-established firms that would pay them above-average salaries and then train them, but slowly, to become the kind of lawyers that gave those firms their excellent reputations. If they made partner (and not all of them would), that would take five to ten years, with the average being around seven.

The small coterie of Harvard Law–trained partners at the two-year-old firm of Kellogg, Huber, Hansen, et al., decided they would make these highly desirable potential hires an offer they couldn't refuse—they promised them they would get to do real trial work almost immediately, make partner in just a few years, *and*, like a top pro ball prospect, be paid a "signing bonus" of one hundred thousand dollars!

According to founding partner Mark Hansen, "Our sales pitch from the beginning was: 'You'll get to do more here than anywhere else, and we're going to pay you more than anyone else.' We were very successful in recruiting with that. Neil liked that. . . . That was the hiring strategy from the beginning. We wanted as many of these people as we could get. . . . But we also had to explain that the doors could be closed in six months. The clerk bonus was 'eye-poppingly bigger than any other firm, and we ruffled a lot of feathers by doing it. But it worked.'

"Once at Kellogg, Huber, much of Judge Gorsuch's time was dedicated to the firm's telecom clients, working on complex regulatory and antitrust matters springing from the breakup of AT&T. In the early 2000s, he also successfully represented a heavily indebted D.C. hospital in a dispute with insurance carriers and was on the plaintiffs' side in a 'payday loan' class action."

Another Kellogg, Huber partner, Steven Benz, who helped recruit Gorsuch, told the legal blog *Law360* that the firm was unusual in that it represented both plaintiffs and defendants, which meant a broader range of experience for the new hires: "At our firm, Neil experienced what it's like to litigate a case from start to finish, and he's lived the difficulties of civil discovery. He's experienced life in the litigation trenches."

★

"AS A PRIVATE-SECTOR ATTORNEY, Gorsuch could have practiced with any large corporate law firm in the United States, but instead chose a small firm in its very early days—a riskier path, to be sure." So wrote David C. Frederick, also a partner in the firm that today is called Kellogg, Hansen, Todd, Fiegel & Frederick. Mr. Frederick called Gorsuch "brilliant, diligent, open-minded and thoughtful."

In his decade at Kellogg, Huber, Neil Gorsuch represented both plaintiffs and defendants, sued as well as defended large corporations, and represented the U.S. Chamber of Commerce, but also filed and won class-action lawsuits for groups of consumers. But the case that Frederick remembers best is one that Gorsuch "brought" to the firm after he'd left to become a federal appellate court judge in Denver.

Frederick wrote:

> Some years ago, he called me about a case he had reviewed on the 10th Circuit's motions docket involving an Arab Muslim incarcerated in a state prison. The guards allegedly called the inmate "9/11" and mistreated him during his confinement. The district court had rejected the inmate's claim that his constitutional rights had been violated and dismissed his lawsuit.
>
> Over the phone, though, Gorsuch explained that he thought the plaintiff prisoner might have a valid claim, but couldn't tell for sure. He asked our law firm to represent the inmate, which I agreed to do so long as a younger colleague could be the principal lawyer on the case and argue under my supervision. Gorsuch agreed and then recused himself from the case to avoid an appearance of conflict. My associate, Janie Nitze, later won a reversal by the 10th Circuit, which reinstated the prisoner's claims. That man got his day in court because of Gorsuch's conscientious approach to judging.

★

ATTORNEY WAN KIM, A Kellogg, Hansen partner currently on sab-batical, who worked with Neil Gorsuch both at the firm and at DOJ, recalls life at the start-up boutique. "I joined the firm in early 1997"—Gorsuch had been there since 1995—"because the job I'd had at DOJ convinced me I really wanted more courtroom experience."

Gorsuch and Kim had taken similar but different routes to arrive at Kellogg, Huber (then, but since 2000, Kellogg, Hansen). After law school graduation from the University of Chicago, Wan Kim clerked for a year for Judge John Buckley of the Court of Appeals for the D.C. Circuit and then went to the Justice Department as part of its honors program, where he was the assistant attorney general in the Civil Rights Division in 2007, when he left to join Kellogg, Huber. Gorsuch came to the firm directly from his second Supreme Court clerk-ship, the first with Byron White and later with Anthony Kennedy.

While Kim says that young lawyers at Kellogg, Huber got more trial experience there than did their counterparts at the big well-known firms, he left after two years to rejoin Justice as an assistant U.S. attorney for D.C., where he was guaranteed to get an even greater amount of courtroom work. (Along the way he also served as counsel to the Senate Judiciary Committee.)

"At that time, the firm did both litigation and telecom, and Neil and I both worked as litigators, and we got along quite well. The practice of law at that law firm was better than I thought it would be coming out of law school."

★

NOT ONLY DID MARK Hansen recruit Gorsuch, but he worked closely with him for the decade Gorsuch was part of the firm.

At the time of Gorsuch's nomination to the Supreme Court, Hansen told Bureau of National Affairs reporter Rebecca Breyer that Gorsuch was "a very skilled attorney. He loved the practice of law. He was very practical, not just an ivory tower, lofty intellectual. He was good at learning the facts, good at dealing with clients and adversaries— an all-around fine lawyer." It took Gorsuch just two years to make partner at Kellogg, Huber, which would have been impossible at an average Big Law firm but was fairly routine at Kellogg, Huber.

While there, Gorsuch tried a variety of cases for a variety of clients, large and small, well-known as well as unknown. One Virginia civil case involved the fashion and home furnishings company Laura Ashley. Sir Bernard Ashley's financial advisors had talked him into investing in Keswick Hall, a failing real estate development near Charlottesville, Virginia.

During his pretrial preparation, Gorsuch deposed a reputedly knowledgeable witness who represented Coopers & Lybrand, Keswick's accounting firm. For the entire eight hours of the deposition, the witness's only answer to Gorsuch's questions was "I don't know." Gorsuch turned the tables on Keswick's lawyers by using the eight-hour string of "I don't knows" as evidence to support an earlier ruling by the judge, a move that precluded the company from using most of the arguments it had planned to use at trial. The case settled, in a confidential agreement, on what would have been the first day of trial.

Mark Hansen wrote that both Sir Bernard and his French wife "Regine—Lady Ashley to us—took to Neil immediately. Watching Neil amble down the long hallway at Keswick Hall, B.A.'s country house hotel, Lady Ashley turned to me and remarked, in a heavy French accent, 'That Neil, he is very ambitious.' She meant it in a good way."

Hansen also wrote: "Neil had a knack for understanding clients and establishing relationships that led them to trust him. And so it was that Neil found himself, less than a year into practice, examining key witnesses and arguing critical motions in B.A.'s case before the Albemarle County [Virginia] Circuit Court—on his own, no hand-holder there to prompt him.

Even the losers saluted Gorsuch's performance. Donald R. Morin, the Charlottesville, Virginia, lawyer who opposed Gorsuch in that case, had high praise for the young lawyer from Kellogg, Huber. His work was "of the highest legal and ethical quality. He made it extremely tough for the defense, and his ethics were unquestionable. If he told you something, you definitely could believe it."

According to former partner David C. Frederick's March 8, 2017, *Washington Post* op-ed article ("There is no principled reason to vote against Gorsuch"), "Anyone who sees Gorsuch as [being] automatically pro-corporation should talk to the officers at Rockwell International and Dow Chemical, against whom he reinstated a $920 million jury verdict for environmental contamination at the Rocky Flats nuclear facility. Executives at U.S. Tobacco Company might also be wringing their hands at the moment, given that Gorsuch, as an attorney, helped to attain one of the largest antitrust verdicts in history against the company."

In March 2017, the *Stanford Law Review* published two essays about Gorsuch. One was by a judge who'd sat on the Tenth Circuit Court of Appeals with Gorsuch (before leaving to teach law at Stanford), and the other was by Mark Hansen, who wrote:

Neil joined a firm that was only about two years old. . . .
It was a far cry from Columbia, Harvard, and Oxford. He
had come to learn to be a lawyer. . . . Not for him the quiet
library carrel: he wanted to be *out there*, helping clients, con-

tending with adversaries, and arguing to courts. He accepted assignments willingly and did them well. He pitched in when—as was often the case—we were overwhelmed with the demands of high stakes litigation. Neil was, for partners, the kind of associate you prize; for associates, the kind of colleague you enjoy working alongside; and for clients, the young, eager, and committed lawyer who inspires both affection and confidence.

One of the most appreciative clients mentioned by Hansen in his article was Sir Bernard Ashley in the Virginia civil case discussed earlier. Hansen writes that Sir Bernard was a larger-than-life figure: "A robust six feet, four inches tall with an even larger personality, a commanding man who loved to hold court. Over tea he would tell wonderful stories of life in the famed Gurkha regiment of the British army and then as an entrepreneur bicycling printed tea towels over to Harrods. He and the eponymous Laura built a fashion empire that produced the largest IPO ever floated on the London Stock Exchange."

When it came time to argue the defendant's motion for reconsideration, the hearing ran deep into the night on the day before trial before a packed audience. "There, in the packed, elegant colonial-style courtroom, the author of Virginia's leading civil procedure treatise warned the judge that the wily Gorsuch had led him into fatal error. But the judge stuck to his ruling; the Virginia Supreme Court denied the defendant's emergency mandamus petition; and the case settled the next day," the day trial was to begin.

In the penultimate paragraph of his Stanford essay, Hansen reminisced: "The following years brought other colorful and memorable trials, such [as] the month-long *Conwood* case in the Western District of Kentucky before the Honorable Thomas B. Russell and a jury of twelve. The result: the largest judgment ever affirmed and collected under the federal antitrust laws. . . . [T]he case was won by a team of four lawyers. We worked from an abandoned Elks Lodge just a shout across the alley from the tiny federal courthouse in Paducah."

THE HEADLINE IN THE March 14, 2017, *New York Times* read "Neil Gorsuch has web of ties to secretive billionaire." While the body of the article itself failed to live up to the provocative implications of the headline by revealing nothing untoward, it raised the question of the identity of the "secretive billionaire." His name turned out to be Philip Anschutz, and he had already generated media interest unrelated to his being a client of the Supreme Court nominee. In California and the western states, he was well-known, and so publicity averse that he was called "the anti-Trump."

To call Philip Anschutz rich and successful is like calling Kareem Abdul-Jabbar tall and talented. At one point he was the seventh-richest man in America; today he has backslid to a mere thirty-ninth. When he sat down with Ben Ryder Howe of *Town & Country* magazine in 2017, it was the seventy-seven-year-old mogul's first-ever lengthy interview:

> If you've been to a concert recently by Taylor Swift, Kanye West, or Justin Bieber, you put money in his pocket. If you've been to Yellowstone National Park, Mount Rushmore, or the Grand Canyon, your dollars likely found their way to him. Chances are you've heard of the basketball team he co-owns, the Los Angeles Lakers, or the railroad he used to hold, the

Southern Pacific. It's possible that today you will start the morning by reading one of his newspapers, drive to work in a car fueled by oil from one of his wells, and at night catch a Hollywood blockbuster he produced in one of the hundreds of movie theaters he owns, followed by a T-bone raised on one of his ranches.

Gorsuch and Anschutz met when the latter hired Kellogg, Huber to represent him in a civil matter in Colorado. Eventually, Gorsuch became his personal attorney and mentee. When President George W. Bush was looking to name federal appellate court judges in the West, Anschutz, a major Republican donor, lobbied hard, and successfully, for Neil Gorsuch.

A 2012 article (by Connie Bruck) in *The New Yorker* entitled "The Man Who Owns L.A." provides numerous details about Anschutz:

Philip Anschutz, who is seventy-two, owns A.E.G. [Anschutz Entertainment Group] [and] has an estimated net worth of seven billion dollars, according to *Forbes.* He has made his fortune in oil and gas, real estate, railroads, telecommunications, and sports and entertainment. He is one of the largest landowners in the U.S., and his empire of more than a hundred and fifty companies, nearly all privately held, is worldwide. He is philanthropically active and has donated more than a hundred million dollars to create the Anschutz Medical Campus, at the University of Colorado, in Aurora. But Anschutz, who lives in Denver, is intensely private and does little to publicize his ownership of A.E.G. or any of his other business activities.

Bruck writes further that when Anschutz visits Los Angeles, he comes alone, sans entourage: "Friends say that the larger the gathering the more quiet Anschutz becomes. . . . Such self-effacement has created some bafflement in a city that takes personal aggrandizement for granted. According to Steve Soboroff, a businessman who was an adviser to former Mayor Richard Riordan during the building of Staples Center, 'Anschutz . . . is the most important Angeleno of the last fifty years, and he's not even an Angeleno.'"

Gorsuch began representing Anschutz and his companies when he was working for Kellogg, Huber. Mark Hansen said he assigned the future judge, then a junior partner, to help on various cases involving the Anschutz Company "both because of his skills and experience and because he had expressed to me an interest in getting involved in things relating to his home state."

THE LONGER GORSUCH STAYED at Kellogg, Huber, the more diverse his practice became. As he told the Senate Judiciary Committee in a written statement in 2006 when he was named to the Tenth Circuit Court of Appeals, "During my time in private practice, I was involved in matters large and small for clients ranging from individuals to non-profits to corporations; my cases ranged from simple breach of contract disputes to complex anti-trust, RICO, and securities fraud matters. I tried cases, participated in substantial injunctive and evidentiary hearings, and argued motions of all kinds, including case dispositive motions to dismiss and for summary judgment. Discovery disputes, *in limine* motions in preparation for trial, post-trial motions, etc. I also took and defended depositions regularly, worked on appeals before federal and state courts of appeal across the country, and provided antitrust and other legal counsel to clients. I estimate that, during my time in private practice, roughly 70% of my litigated matters were in federal court and 30% in state courts. Approximately 90% of these matters involved civil disputes, with the remainder involving criminal matters."

★

AT THE TIME OF his nomination, one of the main raps against Neil Gorsuch was that, à la his hero Antonin Scalia, he favored large corporations, i.e., the big guy over the little guy. However, a closer look at his record as a judge suggests that this assumption may be based on insufficient evidence.

In an article for *The Atlantic* magazine entitled "A Supreme Court Nominee Alert to the Dangers of Big Business," the prolific legal writer Jeffrey Rosen, professor of law at George Washington University and a contributing editor to *The Atlantic*, writes that both Gorsuch proponents and opponents might well be in for a surprise or two if they took a closer look at his rulings on antitrust matters.

Rosen begins his lengthy article by taking issue with the Gorsuch-is-for-the-big-guy positions of Senator Chuck Schumer, the Center for American Progress, and the Constitutional Accountability Center, writing that "Gorsuch's supporters respond, plausibly, that in many of the cases in which he ruled on behalf of corporations or against workers, he was following the letter of the law, or was bound by Supreme Court precedents."

On antitrust, Rosen says, "Gorsuch's record is more interesting than his critics allow." And Rosen goes further, suggesting that Gorsuch will not be an easily predictable member of the highest court: "This perspective differs dramatically from the late Justice Antonin

Scalia's views on antitrust. In his own confirmation hearings in 1986, Scalia joked that in law school, he 'never understood' antitrust law, and later learned that he 'should not have understood it because it did not make any sense then.' . . . Gorsuch, by contrast, approaches antitrust law from the perspective of an experienced litigator, not an ideological law professor."

According to Rosen, "As Gorsuch's former law partner, Mark C. Hansen, told *Law360*, the experience in the American Tobacco case gave Gorsuch sensitivity to the perspective of both sides in antitrust cases. 'I don't think he's afraid of antitrust; he understands it and is comfortable with it,' Hansen said. 'He's quite familiar with both sides of the v. in the antitrust world.'"

Like Hansen, Rosen cites Gorsuch's work in 2002 as a lawyer in private practice when he won "what was then the largest affirmed antitrust verdict in American history, a $1.05 billion verdict against the American Tobacco Company. . . . And on the 10th Circuit, Gorsuch wrote three important antitrust opinions that favored big corporations in some cases and their smaller competitors in others."

JEFFREY ROSEN'S ARTICLE IN the March 2017 *Atlantic* was the second long article he had written about Neil Gorsuch. In the previous issue, which came out shortly after Gorsuch was nominated, he had written "A Jeffersonian for the Supreme Court," in which he compared and contrasted Gorsuch with the late justice Antonin Scalia.

According to Rosen: "Neil Gorsuch, President Donald Trump's nominee for the Supreme Court, is one of the most respected conservative legal intellectuals on the federal bench. Like Justice Antonin Scalia, he has the ability and the ambition to lead America's constitutional debate by following a clear vision of textualism and originalism, based on the premise that judges should separate their political from their constitutional conclusions.

"But unlike the Hamiltonian Justice Scalia, the more Jeffersonian Gorsuch seems more willing to return to constitutional first principles and to question the constitutional underpinnings of the post–New Deal administrative state.

"There's no doubt, however, that the principled Gorsuch would be willing to rule against Trump or a Republican Congress if he felt they exceeded their constitutional bounds—if Trump issued executive orders that clashed with the text of federal immigration laws, for example, or if Congress passed laws banning abortions that don't involve crossing state lines and that exceeded its power to regulate interstate commerce. As Gorsuch said at the White House while accepting Trump's nomination, 'A judge who likes every outcome he reaches is very likely a bad judge.'"

Thus it remains to be seen if Neil Gorsuch, now a Supreme Court justice for life, will make decisions that are consistently conservative, like those of the late Scalia or the currently serving Clarence Thomas, or will on occasion surprise people, in the manner of Justice Kennedy and, every once in a while, Chief Justice John Roberts.

Chapter Six

A YEAR AT DOJ

By 2005, Neil Gorsuch was such a valuable partner in the law firm of Kellogg, Huber that when he left, one publication labeled him a "billings juggernaut," meaning he brought a great deal of business—and money—into the firm each year.

In a 2017 speech to the Heritage Foundation, Gorsuch's former partner Mark Hansen verified this statement. He said that as a private lawyer Gorsuch, whom he called a "constitutionally hard worker," had between 2,400 and 3,000 billable hours, and that he had maintained that output for seven years. Hansen knew this to be a fact, he said, because he had personally reviewed Gorsuch's billing entries at the firm. (According to the National Association for Law Placement, "billable hours requirements [for associates] ranged from 1,400 to 2,400 hours per year in 2004, [with] most offices reporting a minimum [requirement of] either 1,800 or 1,900 hours.")

"That's a lot," said Hansen, who dismissed out of hand any notion that forty-nine-year-old Gorsuch couldn't handle the caseload of the nation's top bench. Hansen said that Gorsuch possessed "a great talent for civil trial law" and would have had a "lucrative" career had he not gone into public service.

"I would argue today that that experience as a civil trial lawyer, working in the trenches of our court system, is as telling about what

Neil could be like as a justice as anything perhaps other than his service as an actual judge."

At Heritage, Hansen also said, "I think it's fair to say that Neil's deep and lengthy engagement with our civil justice system exceeds that of any nominee to the United States Supreme Court since John Paul Stevens in 1975."

Hansen also debunked the charge from the left that Gorsuch was a friend of big corporations and a foe of the "little guy," citing the payday loans case in which numerous little guys had ended up with interest rates of 400 percent, stating, "I remember how deeply Neil . . . felt about trying to get justice for this woman and the other people who'd been victimized by this scheme."

But the Justice Department had beckoned at a time when the young lawyer was looking to flesh out his resume to include public service. According to Wan Kim, with whom Gorsuch worked at both the firm and the Department of Justice, "Neil was highly valued at the firm, but there came a time when he decided he wanted to serve the public, to do public service. He had done quite well at the firm, but he wanted to serve the public."

Asked if he thought Gorsuch saw DOJ as a stepping-stone to the federal bench, or if he had been motivated by his mother's example, Kim quickly says no. "That's certainly not what he talked about. He simply went there with no other agenda than serving the public. We talked about the job several times while we were there, and it was clear that he really enjoyed what he was doing."

When Gorsuch was nominated for the Supreme Court, numerous media outlets described him as having been the "number three man in the Justice Department," but Wan Kim says that's not quite accurate. "He was the Principal Deputy to the Assistant Attorney General

Robert McCallum. He was Robert McCallum's number one aide, and when Robert was not around Neil would be the Acting Assistant General, and in that case it would be accurate. But I don't think most people would call the Principal Deputy the same as the Assistant Attorney General.

"Neil was very smart, very earnest, and very hardworking. He and I had gotten along well at Kellogg Huber. It was a firm that was very intense, and it was staffed with very young lawyers, both the partners and the associates. And all were top rate—but I'm a little bit biased. The firm had made an effort to recruit people who were quite qualified, but Neil stood out."

Also serving with Gorsuch at the Department of Justice was attorney Lily Fu Claffee, today the senior vice president, chief legal officer, and general counsel of the U.S. Chamber of Commerce (as well as executive vice president of the Chamber's Litigation Center).

"When we went to Justice, the job description was to oversee its civil litigating component. When you are in a leadership role your job is not to talk down and second guess the litigating decisions of the litigating component, but rather to provide guidance and strategic direction.

"Traditionally, the Associate Attorney General is very closely aligned with the president and the White House. It's a way the president can give executive direction to that part of the Justice Department without having to have everything go through the Attorney General. And when we were there, Robert McCallum was a very close ally of George W. Bush. It wasn't like the president was calling McCallum every day; the White House wasn't run like that back then. But we knew that whatever Robert wanted was closely aligned with what the president would have wanted us to do.

"It was a great relationship. We had very close relations with the other people who were in leadership positions and in the other litigating division, so it was an extremely collegial type of relationship."

At the time she joined the Justice Department, Ms. Claffee was an equity partner with the Chicago firm Mayer, Brown, and she says that while she loved the firm, "When you're in a big firm there aren't that many opportunities to do something meaningful outside of your law firm work. So when something comes along like that—the chance to run one of the most important agencies in the federal government—how fun! And it's litigation, so you know what you're talking about. In my practice at Mayer Brown, I frequently had the government on 'the other side of the v' from me. So this was an opportunity to see how the other side lives."

Claffee sees Gorsuch's reasons as similar but not identical. "Neil was so well-established at his own firm, so well-regarded, and was making so much money that I don't see his motivation as the same as mine. I saw it as a career opportunity. Also I knew how well-regarded Robert McCallum was at the Justice Department, and how close he was to the president. So for me it was an important opportunity to work with Robert, and I think that was true for Neil, too. He really looked up to Robert, and I think he saw that—working with McCallum—as a way to enhance his career and his resume [by being] in government."

With regard to Gorsuch's being named to the federal bench, Claffee sees it as simply serendipitous, because "no one can really plan for it. These things come up when they come up, but when a lawyer gets the nod, especially one who has been successful in private practice, there's a good deal of ambivalence involved in making the decision. I knew how prominent he was and his family was in Denver, so I thought it made a lot of sense. Especially for lawyers like him who are, to use my own adjective, 'appellatey' [her term for a lawyer who is good at appellate work as well as—or as opposed to—trials], which he is, though he's also a trial lawyer, but because he clerked for the Supreme Court, I'd include him in that definition.

"But all of us lawyers have this hesitation about being considered for a judicial job. It's very monastic—and you earn a government fixed salary for the rest of your life. If you're going to be a federal judge, the administration wants you to do it for life. They don't want you to do it for a year. So, if you're a young lawyer with great earning potential and may want to have other chapters in your life, it's kind of a difficult thing to be asked if you want this monastic existence for the rest of your life and have the same colleagues for the rest of your life. And he was 39. So, a difficult question.

"Some people think being a judge is a gold ring, but it's actually a big commitment. Not all that glitters is gold. Now there are some lawyers who are perfectly suited for it. But Neil, he could be anything—he could be King of the universe! He had no idea he was going to end up on the Supreme Court. But he thought about it, and said, 'Okay, I'll do it for the rest of my life.'"

In 2005, the year Neil Gorsuch arrived at Justice, the aftershocks of 9/11 were still being felt. The DOJ's inspector general had issued a report listing counterterrorism as its "top management and performance challenge": "The highest priority of the Department of Justice continues to be its efforts to deter, prevent, and detect future terrorist acts. Given the importance of this ongoing challenge, a significant amount of the Office of the Inspector General's (OIG) oversight efforts in the 4 years since September 11, 2001, have focused on Department programs and operations related to counter-terrorism and national security issues."

In 2006, while Neil Gorsuch worked at Justice, President George

W. Bush appointed Alberto Gonzales as the attorney general of the United States, to succeed John Ashcroft (the former governor of and senator from Missouri), who, in November, had resigned effective the day his successor was confirmed by the Senate. (Several years later he founded the Ashcroft Group, a Washington, D.C., lobbying firm, which soon became highly successful.)

At the time of Ashcroft's leaving the cabinet, the *New York Times* wrote, "Mr. Ashcroft's resignation will end one of the more controversial tenures in the attorney general's office in recent decades. Mr. Ashcroft presided over the Justice Department in a time of crisis and bitter debate over the balance between national security and individual liberty that followed the terrorist attacks of Sept. 11, 2001. To his admirers, Mr. Ashcroft was a tireless and incorruptible law enforcer determined to protect the country and unafraid of criticism from civil libertarians. To his critics, he has been willing to skirt or trample upon the Constitution to fulfill his and President Bush's concept of national security."

Before becoming attorney general, Gonzales had also been in the news. In March 2004, Ashcroft's Justice Department had ruled that the domestic intelligence program known as Stellar Wind, a warrantless surveillance program begun under George W. Bush, was illegal. The day after the ruling, Ashcroft had an attack of acute pancreatitis and was taken to the hospital. President Bush sent Alberto Gonzales, then the White House Counsel, and Andrew Card, his chief of staff, to get Ashcroft to sign a document reversing the Justice Department's ruling, but the semiconscious Ashcroft, backed up by Acting Attorney General James Comey and Jack Goldsmith, head of the DOJ Office of Legal Counsel, refused to sign, and the ruling stood.

Both Bush and Gonzales were heavily criticized for their part in this effort, Bush for issuing the order and Gonzales for being willing to carry it out.

★

GONZALES'S TENURE AS ATTORNEY general, while less contentious than Ashcroft's, was hardly trouble free. Critics faulted him for his policy of warrantless searches of American citizens and for authorizing "enhanced interrogation techniques," which were used on prisoners held at Guantanamo Bay (nicknamed Gitmo). It was this latter area in which Neil Gorsuch spent a good deal of time and effort during his short stint at the DOJ.

In 2006, when he was nominated and confirmed (unanimously) for the federal bench, Gorsuch was not questioned about his year at the Department of Justice, but in 2017, in his Supreme Court confirmation hearings, quite a bit of time was devoted to his work at Justice, in particular his efforts in relation to the prison at Guantanamo Bay, specifically the memos he wrote relating to the legal basis of the administration's actions regarding the prison. And many of the questions submitted for the record after the Gorsuch hearings were finished—but before the vote on his nomination—also had to do with his DOJ year, which was of particular interest to Democrats, especially Dianne Feinstein and Richard Durbin, the ranking minority member and the minority whip, respectively.

On Thursday, March 9, 2017, eleven days before the Judiciary Committee hearings were to begin, Samuel Ramer, the acting assistant attorney general, released to the committee 144,000 pages of internal DOJ documents relating to Neil Gorsuch. In a cover letter he explained that while the material normally would have been exempt from disclosure under the Freedom of Information Act rules, he was making an exemption to "accommodate" the committee. (While this was not unprecedented, the number of documents was unusually large. According to a White House spokesperson, it was "one of the most transparent processes in nomination history.")

In a separate letter, Mr. Ramer informed Senator Feinstein that Gorsuch had been part of a Department of Justice team that handled the case of *ACLU* v. *DOD*, in which the American Civil Liberties Union had filed a Freedom of Information suit against the Department of Defense in an attempt to get the government to release photos of the prisoners at Gitmo, which they believed would show that the prisoners had been and were being mistreated.

The documents were relevant to the Judiciary Committee's inquiry for two reasons: One, Gorsuch had drafted comments on the case; and two, he had been sent to Guantanamo by DOJ to see if the allegations were true.

Reporting for *Law360* on April 7, 2017, Michael Macagnone wrote:

> During his tenure at the U.S. Department of Justice, Supreme Court nominee Judge Neil Gorsuch worked on talking points and other documents in response to a high court decision on Guantanamo Bay detainees, documents released this week show. Judge Gorsuch, then a principal deputy to former Attorney General Alberto Gonzales, circulated draft interagency talking points in response to the Supreme Court's June 2006 decision in *Hamdan* v. *Rumsfeld* and wrote part of Gonzales' testimony submitted to the Senate Judiciary Committee on the case.
>
> The documents [which were the common effort of several attorneys and were not signed by any one individual] amplify a Thursday letter from acting Assistant Attorney General

Samuel Ramer that said Judge Gorsuch, who serves on the Tenth Circuit, had played an active role in the Hamdan case, which involved terror kingpin Osama bin Laden's former chauffeur. The DOJ defended the Bush administration's military commissions tasked with charging Guantanamo Bay detainees. Gorsuch discussed litigation options, reviewed pleadings and developed strategy in the case, the letter said.

At his confirmation hearings, Gorsuch was asked, by Illinois senator Dick Durbin, "Would you put in perspective any comments that you made about people representing Guantanamo detainees?" Durbin was referring to a comment Gorsuch had made about lawyers from "elite law firms" representing some Guantanamo detainees pro bono. Gorsuch replied, "I have nothing but admiration for those lawyers. The email you are referring to is not my finest moment. [I was] blowing off steam with a friend privately. The truth is, I think my career is better than that. When I have seen individuals who have needed representation, as a judge when I have gotten handwritten pro se filing, [when] I have seen something that might have merit in it, I picked up the phone and have gotten a lawyer for that person. . . . I would like to think that my career taken as a whole, Senator, represents my values appropriately."

The email containing the draft talking points said that Al Qaeda detainees would not receive full prisoner-of-war protection from the Department of Defense and that the Supreme Court decision did not require that treatment. Other emails said that a final version of the talking points would be shared with other agencies.

According to the common draft, "[The Guantanamo prisoners] have nothing but contempt for the laws of war and the Geneva Conventions. They kidnap relief aid workers, behead contractors, journalists, and U.S. military personnel, and bomb religious shrines, wedding parties, and restaurants. They openly mock the rule of law, the Geneva Conventions, and the standards of civilized people everywhere."

Because Gorsuch was working as part of a team, the extent of his written contributions to these letters and talking points is not clear. What is clear, however, is that the Department of Justice sent Gorsuch to Guantanamo Bay to check on the treatment of the prisoners. Upon his return, the future judge sent General Jay W. Hood, the commander, a letter thanking him for showing him around the prison: "I was extraordinarily impressed. You and your colleagues have developed standards and imposed a degree of professionalism that the nation can be proud of, and being able to see firsthand all that you have managed to accomplish with such a difficult and sensitive mission makes my job of helping explain and defend it before the courts all the easier."

Several months later, Gorsuch took a further step, suggesting, in an interdepartmental memo, that federal judges should visit Gitmo in order to better understand the Bush administration's "litigating positions." Specifically, he wrote that such a visit—"or even just the offer of a visit"—would "dispel myths and build confidence in our representations to the Court about conditions and detainee treatment. . . . If the DC judges could see what we saw, I believe they would be more sympathetic to our litigating positions."

The *Law360* article continues:

But while Judge Gorsuch spent those 14 months immersed in executive power and national security disputes from the Bush administration's perspective, his own comments in the documents rarely sounded overtly ideological notes. . . . Peter Keisler, who worked with Judge Gorsuch on several such matters as the head of the Civil Division at the time, argued that [Gorsuch's] role during that period should be understood as representing a client: He helped shape arguments and litigation strategy, but not the underlying national security policy decisions which "had already been made. . . . The emails just reflect the fact that he was gratified when the department would win and disappointed when it would lose, which is not surprising because these were cases he was working on as an attorney for the government and advancing its positions," Mr. Keisler said.

IN 2001, SALIM AHMED Hamdan, a Yemeni national often described as a driver for Osama bin Laden, while attempting to return to Yemen, was arrested by the Northern Alliance in Afghanistan, who turned him over to the U.S. military (for bounty). Hamdan was charged with one count of conspiring against U.S. citizens. He said he was just a former chauffeur, but the government said he was a terrorist.

Hamdan sued on the theory that the commission set up to try Guantanamo detainees was not legal. The D.C. Court of Appeals found for the government, but the Supreme Court reversed that decision by a vote of five to three, with Chief Justice Roberts having recused himself.

The work that Neil Gorsuch did on this case supported the government's position that the president had the necessary authority under the Use of Military Force Act, which had been passed following the attacks of September 11, 2001. The government claimed that Hamdan and the other prisoners were "unlawful combatants," not prisoners of war, and therefore not entitled to the protection of the Geneva Conventions.

On June 30, 2017, *Law360* reported, "In addition, the talking points noted that the conditions at the prison at the Naval base at Guantanamo Bay already complied with Article 3 of the Convention and that the Supreme Court case only extended to applying the Geneva Conventions as a matter of law and to the extent that they applied to the legal foundation of the military commissions. The documents, submitted to the Senate Judiciary Committee by the DOJ this week, do not include any other DOJ drafts of the talking points or the final document, so it is uncertain how much of the final product Gorsuch wrote."

Senator Dianne Feinstein's questions for the record during the confirmation hearings in 2017 began with Gorsuch's work on the Hamdan case.

The California Democrat's first question was preceded by this partial statement:

> At your hearing, you acknowledged you worked on the
> Graham amendment to the Detainee Treatment Act, which
> sought to eliminate habeas corpus for Guantanamo detain-
> ees. You also acknowledged that in December 2005, after
> the Detainee Treatment Act was passed, there were different
> factions in the administration advocating different versions of
> the signing statement. . . . I read your email as saying if the
> administration issued a signing statement along these lines
> then the passage of the McCain amendment would not re-
> quire much of a change in interrogation policy than what the
> Department of Justice had already decided was allowable.

She then asked, "What did your email mean?," and Gorsuch replied, "The December 29, 2005, email chain discussed proposed versions of a signing statement to accompany the Detainee Treatment

Act. As we discussed at the hearing, these events took place many years ago and my recollection is that there were individuals in maybe the Vice President's office who wanted a more aggressive signing statement . . . and that there were others, including at the State Department, who wanted a gentler signing statement. To my recollection, as I said at the hearing, I was in the latter camp. . . . I did so in my role as a lawyer helping with civil litigation brought by individuals detained as enemy combatants and defended by the Department of Justice. The email chain indicates that the Legal Adviser for the State Department favored a gentler and more expansive statement for various reasons, including public and foreign relations. The email chain also indicates that the National Security Council expressed the view that the Detainee Treatment Act codified existing policies. In that light and as a lawyer advising a client, the email chain indicates that I suggested a signing statement could (1) speak about the Detainee Treatment Act positively to the public . . . foreign nations as the State Department suggested, (2) highlight aspects of the legislation helpful to litigators in the Civil Division of the Department of Justice, and (3) make transparent the client's position that the Act codified existing policies."

One of Senator Feinstein's next questions had to do with the highly controversial topic of waterboarding. "On the first day of questioning, you told Senator Graham that the Detainee Treatment Act prohibits waterboarding. But an email you wrote when you were part of the Bush administration Justice Department seems to say the opposite—you said that the law should be read as 'essentially codifying interrogation practices,' which at the time included waterboarding, stress positions, sleep deprivation, and other techniques that had been approved in the Bradbury OLC memo from 2005. . . . When did you come to the view that the Detainee Treatment Act bars waterboarding, and why in the Bush administration did you have a different view?"

The nominee answered, "I do not currently recall when precisely I came to that view. By its express terms, the Detainee Treatment Act prohibits cruel, inhuman, and degrading treatment."

Senator Feinstein then moved to a broader type of question: "Do you understand and agree that your former role at the Justice Department—and the positions you advocated for while at the Justice Department on behalf of the government—can and should have no bearing on the way you decide cases as a judge?"

Gorsuch did agree, and said so: "I understand and agree that my former role at the Department of Justice has not had and will not have any bearing on the way I decide cases as a judge."

The next question was "Why did you see it as a victory that those who might have been tortured or who were detained unlawfully could not exercise their rights to have their habeas claims before a federal court?" (The right of *habeas corpus*, Latin for "Show us the body," is a protection afforded all American citizens under the Constitution that guards them against false imprisonment by guaranteeing that they will go before a judge or magistrate to determine if they can be released pending trial or kept in jail. International human rights law gives this guarantee to all detainees, but the George Bush administration, in the wake of 9/11, was not honoring it, or doing so with very little speed, in the case of the Guantanamo Bay prisoners.)

Gorsuch responded:

As a lawyer in the Department of Justice, I worked with
the Department of Defense and with Congress and others
in a bipartisan effort to establish a system of rules to govern
litigation brought by individuals detained as enemy com-

batants at Guantanamo Bay, bearing in mind the *Youngstown* formulation discussed above. Among other things, and as Senator Graham spoke about at the hearing, a process was put in place to permit detainees to challenge their status as enemy combatants in Combatant Status Review Tribunals as well as in the United States Court of Appeals for the D.C. Circuit. Some in the administration regarded these legislative provisions as intrusions on the President's powers. In contrast, and with others, I welcomed these developments as consistent with *Youngstown*. That is what I recall I meant by "the administration's upside."

The next question from the ranking minority member of the Judiciary Committee had three parts: "a. Is that true? Yes or no. b. Is it true that you worked on the effort to use the Graham amendment to get the Supreme Court to dismiss the *Hamdan* v. *Rumsfeld* case? c. Isn't it also true that the Supreme Court, in *Hamdan* v. *Rumsfeld*, rejected the position you advocated and held that the Graham amendment did not apply to pending cases?"

Gorsuch responded:

The Civil Division and Office of the Solicitor General of the Department of Justice advanced the position that the Detainee Treatment Act would apply to cases pending on the date of its enactment. As a lawyer for the Department, I supported that position. Ultimately, that position did not prevail in the Supreme Court, with five Justices disagreeing with the Government's position and three Justices agreeing (Chief Justice Roberts took no part in the consideration or decision of the case).

The Supreme Court in *Hamdan* (2006) rejected the administration's position that the Graham amendment barred review of Hamdan's case. An e-mail shows you discussed the decision with reporters, and the next day you [the senators] were drafting legislation to reverse the Court's ruling.

Senator Feinstein then asked, "Is that true? And is it also true that, after the Military Commissions Act of 2006 barred pending habeas petitions by Guantanamo detainees, the Supreme Court found that the law was unconstitutional?"

Gorsuch replied:

My involvement in responding to *Hamdan* was limited. *Hamdan* was decided on June 29, 2006, approximately three weeks before I was confirmed as a judge. The Military Commissions Act was signed on October 17, 2006, months after I left the Department of Justice. Your question references an early draft of the Act that I reviewed but do not recall drafting. As I read it today, that draft would not have barred judicial review but would have sought to channel cases through the judicial-review mechanism of the Detainee Treatment Act. It is true that the Supreme Court some years later in *Boumediene* v. *Bush* (2008) held that certain aspects of the Act did not satisfy the Suspension Clause.

Senator Feinstein had been an able and well-informed questioner, and the nominee an adroit responder, but not a great deal of light was shed—which has become par for the course in Supreme Court confirmation hearings.

★

THE NEXT INTERROGATOR WAS the minority whip, Richard Durbin (D-IL), who also wanted to know about Gorsuch's work on the signing statement for the Detainee Treatment Act. Gorsuch said, "As we discussed at the hearing, these events took place many years ago and my recollection is that there were individuals in maybe the Vice President's office who wanted a more aggressive signing statement . . . and that there were others, including at the State Department, who wanted a gentler signing statement. . . . I was in the latter camp [along with] John Bellinger, among others. I did so in my role as a lawyer helping with civil litigation brought by individuals detained as enemy combatants and defended by the Department of Justice."

Durbin then asked if Gorsuch had been briefed "on the CIA's rendition, detention or interrogation program?" Gorsuch answered yes, but said he did not recall, of the many briefings and various national security clearances during his service at the Department of Justice, "which specific programs or when I was read into them." Senator Durbin then moved on.

Matt Ford, in *The Atlantic*, reported:

Illinois's Dick Durbin tried to persuade Gorsuch to reveal his abortion views by quoting the judge's book on euthanasia, in which he said "the intentional taking of human life by private persons is always wrong." Conservatives have interpreted that line as a signal of Gorsuch's supposed anti-abortion beliefs.

"How could you square that statement with legal abortion?" Durbin asked him. "Senator, as the book explains, the Supreme Court of the United States has held in *Roe* v. *Wade* that a fetus is not a person for purposes of the Fourteenth Amendment, and the book explains that," Gorsuch replied.

"Do you accept that?" Durbin asked.

"That's the law of the land," Gorsuch answered. "I accept the law of the land, senator, yes."

DURING THE POST-HEARINGS PERIOD, Gorsuch had submitted more than seventy pages of written responses to Senate Judiciary Committee members' questions regarding his Supreme Court nomination. Ron Bonjean, a communications specialist who had aided Gorsuch during the confirmation process, told the *Washington Examiner*:

> He participated in the longest hearing of any 21st century nominee that lasted three rounds totaling nearly 20 hours and has met with nearly 80 senators. Judge Gorsuch answered 1,200 questions during his hearing. This is twice as many questions as Justices Sotomayor, Kagan or Ginsburg.
>
> He was given 299 questions for the record by the Democrats, not [the full] Senate Judiciary Committee—the most in recent history of Supreme Court nominees. Gorsuch has answered those questions by providing another 70 pages of written responses. He did all this within six days of receiving the questions in order to give [Senate] Democrats ample time to review the answers prior to the committee vote and floor consideration schedule.

QUESTIONS ABOUT NEIL GORSUCH'S work during his year at the Department of Justice did, like several other exchanges during the nomination hearings, produce a few stray puffs of smoke, but no smoking gun. Some of his answers, like his I-was-a-lawyer-doing-a-job-for-a-client, may have struck his detractors as a tad slippery, but there was no evidence that he was dissembling. He was, after all, a Republican lawyer working for a Republican Justice Department that was advancing and supporting the policies of a Republican president. What else would he have done?

ON MARCH 22, 2017, *New York Daily News* reporter Adam Adelman neatly summarized the confirmation hearing's thrust and parry:

> Gorsuch, appearing again before the Senate Judiciary Committee, was asked to expound upon his job as a lawyer in George W. Bush's Justice Department, where he helped draft certain anti-terrorism measures. Sen. Dianne Feinstein (D-Calif.), the ranking Democrat on the panel, pressed Gorsuch about his role in reviewing, and in some cases, approving, enhanced interrogation tactics, peppering the jurist with questions about a document from early 2006 that asked if "the aggressive interrogation techniques employed by the administration yielded any valuable intelligence" or "ever stopped a terrorist incident?" Gorsuch appears to have written "yes" in the margin of the document. When Feinstein asked him about that position, however, he said he was only doing his "job" as a lawyer for the administration. "My recollection of 12 years ago is that that was the position that the clients were telling us. I was a lawyer. My job was as an advocate, and we were dealing with detainee litigation. That was my job."

Adelman continued:

Feinstein . . . expressed concern to Gorsuch that he had "been able to avoid any specificity like no one I have ever seen before" and . . . when asked to expound upon his job as a lawyer in George W. Bush's Justice Department, where he helped draft certain anti-terrorism measures, he replied, "No one is looking to return us to horse and buggy days" . . . and when it came to abortion, a frequent topic of his hearing the day before, Gorsuch said plainly on Wednesday that he regarded *Roe* v. *Wade*, the landmark 1973 decision that effectively legalized abortion, as "the law of the land" and again offered assurance repeatedly that he respected precedent and judicial independence. "I care about the law, I care deeply about the law and an independent judiciary and following the rules of the law," he said. "And that's the commitment I can make to you, I can't promise you more and I can't guarantee you any less."

As far as any damage being inflicted on Neil Gorsuch by the Democrats' questions regarding the work Gorsuch did while in the George W. Bush Justice Department, when the fight was over, there was not a drop of blood on the ground.

Chapter Seven

ON THE BENCH

In 2006, when President George W. Bush named Neal Gorsuch to the federal bench as an associate justice on the Tenth Circuit Court of Appeals, Gorsuch's former law firm released a statement which read, in part: "Neil had the brightest possible future as a trial lawyer in private practice. When he decided to leave Kellogg Huber Hansen for government service, he left behind a lucrative and successful career in which he would have thrived. His colleagues understood his admirable desire to serve his country, but were very sorry to see him go. Given Neil's enormous legal talent and his distinguished service in government, we were not surprised by his nomination to the U.S. Court of Appeals for the Tenth Circuit."

But gone he was, and in all likelihood, never to return. The time had come to put on a garment he would wear, also in all likelihood, for decades.

On November 20, 2006, Neil M. Gorsuch, in a ceremony known as an investiture, was sworn in as a federal judge by U.S. Supreme Court Justice Anthony Kennedy, Gorsuch's former boss.

Lending a helping hand as the new appellate court judge donned his new black polyester robe for the first time were the judge's daughters, seven-year-old Emma and her five-year-old sister, Belinda. Asked what she thought of the ceremony, Emma said, "It was nice," and went back to her cookie.

Legal Washington, D.C., was well represented that day. In addition to Justice Kennedy, there were a number of people from the Justice Department, including Rachel Brand, Elisebeth Collins Cook, Brett Gerry, Wan Kim, and Gregory Katsas.

Both of Colorado's U.S. senators spoke, as did Mark Hansen of Kellogg, Huber, and the entire *en banc* Tenth Circuit Court of Appeals was there. *Above the Law* ran a short item provided by what it called a "tipster" who added, irreverently, "The Gorsuch clerks showed everyone around Denver and got trashed on consecutive nights. Good times were had by all."

THE PEOPLE WHO ATTENDED the Gorsuch investiture knew what kind of man and what kind of lawyer he was, and had no doubt he would be a fine judge. But to the Tenth Circuit bar—the lawyers from Colorado, Oklahoma, Kansas, New Mexico, Wyoming, and Utah (the states that make up the circuit), plus those from other states who argued cases before the judges of the Tenth Circuit—the young judge with the prematurely gray hair was an unknown quantity. They weren't sure just what to expect.

One of those lawyers was Baine Kerr, a Denver lawyer with a successful litigation practice. Kerr has had only one case before Neil Gorsuch, but it was a memorable one. He calls the 2001 case, *Simpson v. Colorado*, "Colorado's trial of the century."

"This was an extremely high profile case, the Penn State scandal of its time. As a legal case it really was unprecedented. There have been over a thousand articles written about it. There were state grand jury hearings, and Congressional hearings in Washington, D.C. The president of the University [of Colorado] was fired over it, as were the chancellor, the athletic director, and, eventually, the football coach. With all this citizen and media attention, it was anything but your typical appellate argument."

In 2001, Lisa Simpson (the plaintiff's real name) was a sophomore at the University of Colorado. One night in December, she and several girlfriends were drinking in Simpson's off-campus apartment. One of the women, a tutor for the school's football team, said some of her football player friends would be stopping by. Later a large group of players and several high school students whom the school was trying to recruit—sixteen to twenty in all—came to the apartment. Many of them were drunk.

Ms. Simpson, who also was intoxicated, soon went to bed and fell asleep. According to her complaint, she was awakened a short time later by two of the recruits, who were removing her clothing. She said she was then sexually assaulted by several recruits and several of the football players. She also said that another woman, in another bed in the same room, was being sexually assaulted by "at least one football player."

The next day, Simpson's roommate took her to a community hospital, where she reported the sexual assaults to the staff. The roommate also reported the assaults to the university's vice chancellor for student affairs and the university's Office of Victim Assistance. The players were charged with violating the school's code of conduct, but not with sexual assault. No player lost his eligibility.

Lisa Simpson, who had been an honor student in high school, dropped out of school and did not earn a degree.

The case drew national attention. In February 2004 another University of Colorado student told *Sports Illustrated* that she had been raped by a fellow football player. On February 20, the *L.A. Times* wrote:

Almost every day this month has brought a new accusation against the University of Colorado Buffaloes, and Thursday was no different. Police said they are investigating whether a team member sexually assaulted a woman in 2002, the seventh such claim since 1997.

Players also have been accused of offering alcohol and strippers to high school recruits, which has prompted a high-level investigation. Coach Gary Barnett was placed on leave Wednesday night after downplaying an allegation by Katie Hnida, a former Colorado kicker, who said she was assaulted by a teammate. Barnett called her a "terrible" player.

These developments have pushed Colorado to the forefront of a wave of embarrassing incidents involving college athletics. Much of the controversy centers on the way football programs cozy up to high school prospects.

In March, *People* magazine reported: "Simpson's charges . . . were only the first gush in what has become a torrent of bad news for the University and its nationally ranked football program. In the last three months, two other women filed their own suits, alleging that they had also been sexually assaulted that same weekend by football players or recruits. Then in late January, portions of the depositions, complete with graphic details, were leaked to the press. . . . The growing scandal has attracted national attention and renewed the debate over out-of-control athletic programs and even whether some schools are using sex to entice prize recruits. (It's alleged in some student depositions that the high school players brought to Simpson's apartment were told there were women there willing to have sex with them.)"

In early December 2002, Lisa Simpson sued CU in Colorado state court, and two weeks later the university removed the case to federal court. A year later, Anne Gilmore, who had also been in Simpson's apartment on the night in question and also said she had been raped, filed her claim in federal court; the two causes of action were joined as one case headed *Simpson* v. *Colorado*. (Up to that point, to protect their privacy, the women had been referred to, both in open court and in documents, as "Student Trainer A" and "Student Trainer B.")

In response, the university, which had consistently denied all charges, filed a motion for summary judgment. When granted, such motions eliminate the necessity for a trial because the judge has decided there are no "triable issues of fact." Motions for summary judgment are often filed but rarely granted. However, in December 2005, the district court granted the motion, dismissing the case in its entirety and ordering the plaintiffs, Simpson and Gilmore, to pay the university's expenses. It was at this point that the two young women brought attorney Baine Kerr into the case as lead counsel. Kerr was no stranger to the Tenth Circuit Court of Appeals, but it would be his first time going before a panel that included Neil Gorsuch.

"He had been on the court for just a year," Kerr said, in an interview for this book, "or maybe a little more, and all I knew about him was that he had come from Alberto Gonzales's Justice Department. Now my case was a Title IX civil rights case [because the plaintiff worked for CU's Athletic Department], and under Gonzales the Justice Department had really retrenched dramatically on filing civil rights cases.

"All I knew about Judge Gorsuch was that he had been, basically, number two or three at the Justice Department under Gonzales, and I feared that he would have the same attitude toward plaintiffs' civil rights arguments.

"The only other information I had about him was that he was from out here, which I thought was a positive, and I also knew that he had two daughters, which I considered very much of a positive."

On the day the case was heard, the courtroom was packed, with national as well as local media present. When Baine Kerr began to argue why the decision to grant summary judgment should be reversed, he expected he would have fifteen minutes and then the lawyer for the university would have his quarter-hour turn.

"When I finished my fifteen minutes, I said, 'I see that my time is up,' but Gorsuch said, 'Oh, no. keep talking. We want this to be fully aired.'

"I think I was up there for at least forty-five minutes. And then, after the counsel for the university argued for fifteen minutes, they had me up there *again*—for another forty-five minutes. In that afternoon, I must have been up there for two and a half to three hours, which, based on everyone I've talked to, was totally unprecedented.

"Mr. O'Rourke, the lawyer for the other side," Kerr continued, "had expected to have a judge who was friendly to the university, and we were both flabbergasted by how involved and interested Judge Gorsuch was. At one point, when I was arguing, it was almost like a philosophical dialogue about the problem of sexual harassment and rape by football players.

"O'Rourke just got raked over the coals by Neil Gorsuch, just hammered. But I think that he respects Gorsuch a lot. One of the plaintiffs, a nineteen-year-old girl, had gone to the police and told them she'd been raped by a football player. Three days later, the head football coach called her into his office and told her that if she went ahead with her complaint, her life would be 'altered,' ruined. But he did nothing to the player, other than make him run some laps."

Kerr says that while the case was heard by a three-judge panel, it was Gorsuch who did most of the questioning from the bench. "He just raked my opponent over the coals. At one point he said, 'You're not going to stand there, Mr. O'Rourke, and defend the actions of what that football coach did to student trainer A, are you?' and all poor Pat O'Rourke could say was, 'No, judge, I'm not.'"

Baine Kerr's takeaway from the Colorado rape case? "I walked out of there thinking Neil Gorsuch is one of the greatest friends young women could have in the federal judiciary. And I believe that to this day."

He also believes, despite being a liberal Democrat with only a limited range of experience with Gorsuch, that the new justice would not, if given the opportunity, vote to overturn *Roe* v. *Wade:* "He's very innovative and I think he would vote to extend the law in favor of civil rights. He's a man who has daughters and who's very passionate. Women's civil rights seem very dear to him. So, no, I don't think he would."

IN ADDITION TO NEIL Gorsuch, the judicial panel in the Simpson case consisted of judges Harris L. Hartz and Monroe G. McKay. On September 6, 2007, in an opinion written by Judge Hartz, the court announced its decision.

> In our view, the evidence presented to the district court on CU's motion for summary judgment is sufficient to support findings (1) that CU had an official policy of showing high-school football recruits a "good time" on their visits to the CU campus, (2) that the alleged sexual assaults were caused by CU's failure to provide adequate supervision and guidance

to player-hosts chosen to show the football recruits a "good time," and (3) that the likelihood of such misconduct was so obvious that CU's failure was the result of deliberate indifference. We therefore hold that CU was not entitled to summary judgment.

In simpler English, this meant that the appellate court had overturned the decision of the trial court, ruling, in effect, that summary judgment should not have been granted and the case should have been allowed to go to trial because there was sufficient evidence for the jury to find in Simpson's and Gilmore's favor.

On October 10, 2007, the university filed a petition for rehearing, which a month later the entire Tenth Circuit denied. It also denied CU's request that the entire appellate court decide the issue.

The university had a hard decision to make.

On December 5, 2007, the *Denver Post* reported: "The University of Colorado said today that a settlement has been reached in a Title IX lawsuit that was filed after allegations of rape at a party attended by CU football players. Lisa Simpson will receive $2.5 million and a second woman will receive $350,000 under the agreement signed last night by CU president Hank Brown. Brown said agreeing to the settlement 'was a difficult decision, painful in some ways,' but 'in the best interest of the university.'"

In reprising the facts, the newspaper reported, "On Sept. 6, a three-judge panel of the U.S. 10th Circuit Court of Appeals reinstated Simpson's lawsuit, saying that the key question was whether the risk of such an assault during recruiting visits was obvious. The appellate judges—Harris Hartz, Monroe McKay and Neil Gorsuch—said evidence could support such a finding based on widespread reporting of sexual misconduct in college-football programs, including repeated concerns about CU's program."

According to Simpson's lawyer, Baine Kerr, the November 9 ruling meant he was now free to argue that CU had ignored repeated warnings that some of its football players and recruits engaged in sexual assaults, including rape.

In the September ruling reinstating the lawsuit, the three-judge panel noted that in 1989, *Sports Illustrated* magazine had run an article stating that there'd been a number of sexual assaults by CU players. In 1990, two CU football players were charged with sexual assault arising from separate incidents. Then, in 1997, a high school girl alleged that she had been sexually assaulted by a recruit at a party.

In 1998, as a result of all this publicity, then–Boulder district attorney Alex Hunter and Assistant District Attorney Mary Keenan—the current DA—had met with CU officials to express concern about a pattern of sexual misconduct. At the meeting, Keenan expressed concern about women being made available to recruits for sex.

But the court said that after the meeting with Keenan, CU "did little to change its policies or training. . . . Not only was the coaching staff informed of sexual harassment and assault by players, but it responded in ways that were more likely to encourage than eliminate such misconduct."

AT THE TIME HE defended the University of Colorado in the Tenth Circuit Court of Appeals in the Simpson case, university counsel Patrick O'Rourke was employed by the University of Colorado full-time in its in-house litigation department. Before joining the University of Colorado, O'Rourke had been in private practice as a director of the law firm Montgomery Little & McGrew, in Engle-wood, Colorado.

Not surprisingly, Mr. O'Rourke has a clear and vivid memory of the Simpson case. Asked if it's fair to say that while the plaintiffs' lawyers did not expect Neil Gorsuch to be sympathetic, O'Rourke's "side" did, he replied, "Knowing that Judge Gorsuch had been ap-pointed by a Republican president and was thought to be fairly con-servative, we were hopeful that he would be sympathetic to our view of the case. But he didn't have any track record or any prior Title IX cases, so we were speculating, but we really didn't have any way of knowing. He was an unknown quantity.

"As I recall, Judge Hartz was the presiding judge, so he was the one working the clock, but I was a little bit surprised because nor-mally when you're in the Tenth Circuit you get your fifteen minutes and then you sit down, and that's when it started to stretch up around twenty minutes for Baine, I noticed it; but it's not unusual, if the judges have questions, for it to stretch a little bit. I think I was up for thirty-five to forty minutes. Gorsuch was very active, but I think it's fair to say that all three judges on the panel were not shy."

Would Patrick O'Rourke agree with Baine Kerr's statement that Neil Gorsuch gave him, Pat O'Rourke, a hard time?

"Yeah. It was obvious from when I got up that the panel had some real problems with the underlying case and with Judge Blackburn's [summary judgment] order that was in our favor. Judge Gorsuch asked some pretty pointed questions, and I felt from the time I got up that I was on the defensive."

O'Rourke says pointed questions are to be expected when arguing before the appellate courts, but that this case was markedly different. "Normally someone will give you a softball question to take a swing at, but I don't remember many softball questions in that case."

O'Rourke, who had only one other case before Neil Gorsuch in the years since *Simpson* v. *Colorado*, says the judge is well respected among lawyers who argue before the Tenth Circuit, an assessment with which he, personally, agrees. "He's a good judge, and he was very well respected in our legal community, and after the Simpson case he served on the faculty of the law school and taught, so he's pretty well thought of in our parts."

When told that Baine Kerr believes Neil Gorsuch could become one of women's best friends in the federal judiciary, O'Rourke said, "I don't know. Everybody's kind of guessing right now because you can take judges who are on the Tenth Circuit level, and at that point in time they are applying the law as the Supreme Court gives it to them. When people are on the Supreme Court, they are no longer in the same place they were before, and over time you see justices evolve in their thinking."

Patrick O'Rourke feels it's "way too early" to predict that Gorsuch will become one of the great Supreme Court justices, in part because that depends on the cases in which he gets to play a significant role. "Part of what makes a great justice is the cases they get to decide. And certainly he's young enough that he will be on the bench for a long time and probably will get a chance to sit on some really big important cases. So, if he ends up sitting on those cases and gets assigned those opinions he could be a great one. But if John Roberts doesn't assign those opinions to him, who knows how history will unfold? That's one of the mysteries."

As for *Simpson* v. *Colorado*, Patrick O'Rourke says, "It was a fascinating case, and one I'll remember forever—even though I got squashed."

★

As BACKGROUND FOR THE nomination hearings, the Senate Judiciary Committee sent Neil Gorsuch a lengthy questionnaire that asked for his education, employment, and publication history, plus a list of the "ten most significant cases" he had heard during his decade as an appellate court judge. Gorsuch's answers to the questionnaire ran to sixty-eight pages, and revealed that he had decided 3,000 cases (1,800 criminal and 1,200 civil) while on judicial panels of usually three judges, but sometimes more, an impressively high number.

In *Yellowbear* v. *Lampert*, decided in 2014, Andrew Yellowbear, an Arapaho Indian in prison for murder, wanted to use the prison's sweat lodge, and when the prison officials refused, he brought suit, claiming this violated his right to exercise his religious faith. As People for the American Way, a liberal group, reported, "This was not a difficult case, one that was made even easier by the fact that a ruling for Yellowbear would have no impact whatsoever on anyone else's rights. So it is no surprise that judges nominated by three different presidents (Reagan, Bush 43, and Obama) were in agreement. . . . *Yellowbear* was a straightforward case that Gorsuch ruled correctly on. He and his colleagues were smart enough to know that 'due deference' doesn't mean 'blind acceptance.'"

Hobby Lobby v. *Sibelius*, a 2013 case, was one of the most talked-about cases during the Judiciary Committee members' questioning of Gorsuch. In this case, the Greens, the family that owned Mardel, a crafts and Christian bookstore chain, sued the Department of Health and Human Services, claiming that their faith would not allow them to follow the provision of the Affordable Care Act requiring them to provide their employees with health insurance that covered contraceptive devices. They sought an injunction to halt the fines triggered by the noncompliance, and when they lost, they appealed the decision. The question became whether a corporation had this right, and the court claimed a corporation did have that right. Gorsuch, who voted with the majority (but did not write the opinion), noted in a concurrence, as *qz.com* reported, "that the family's views were reprehensible to some and that religious freedom laws are especially designed to protect unpopular positions."

JUDGE GORSUCH'S SELECTION OF these specific cases did not seem de-signed to send any particular message other than to give the commit-tee a representative sampling of decisions, dissents, and concurrences over a broad range of topics. But he did manage to include cases that involved issues dear to him, such as his opposition to the Chevron deference, his support for religious liberty, and his Scalia-like view of the Fourth Amendment prohibition against unreasonable searches and seizures.

Jimmy Hoover of *Law360* wrote in 2017 that Gorsuch had "shed light on his judicial priorities"; Reuters' Allison Frankel commented, "After spending a long day immersed in Judge Gorsuch's rulings, I can confirm one certainty about the judge: He is an elegant writer whose opinions have all the punch of Scalia's but none of the occa-sional nastiness. The law will be a little more broadly accessible if he is confirmed"; and *Washington Post* legal reporter Robert Barnes observed, "[He] is a proponent of originalism—meaning that judges should attempt to interpret the words of the Constitution as they were understood at the time they were written—and a textualist who con-siders only the words of the law being reviewed, not legislators' intent or the consequences of the decision."

Chapter Eight

A WAY WITH WORDS

From his earliest days as a student, Neil Gorsuch—like his legal hero Antonin Scalia—displayed an ability to write well, which he later honed. At Georgetown Prep he wrote occasionally; at Columbia University frequently; less so while in law school; and then considerably more when he turned his Oxford dissertation into his first book, *The Future of Assisted Suicide and Euthanasia*.

But it was during his three years at Columbia (1986–88) that Neil Gorsuch wrote most often and on a fairly regular basis as he and like-minded friends offered a conservative alternative to the liberal views that prevailed at Columbia in the mid-1980s.

The in-your-face conservative arguments that he had offered, politely and with humor, while sparring with liberal professors at Georgetown Prep gave way to more fully formed statements of personal belief intended to sway the opinions of others or simply to vent his disagreement with some of what he considered the more outré opinions of campus liberals.

This became easier to do after Gorsuch and two of his friends, Andrew Levy and P. T. Waters, founded *The Columbia Federalist* as a campus publication with a conservative, satirical bent. This period was also the time when young Neil Gorsuch began to solidify his belief in both originalism as a way of interpreting the U.S. Constitution and textualism as the correct way to read a statute, i.e., by following the exact wording and not looking to the intent of the legislators.

In his first year, he ran for a seat in the student senate. He was disqualified for having put up too many posters, but he had already answered a questionnaire sent to all the candidates by the student newspaper *The Spectator*. The first question had to do with whether the U.S. Marine Corps should be allowed to recruit on campus. Most candidates answered in the negative, citing the Corps' policy of not accepting gay men and women, but Gorsuch took a different tack.

"The question here," he wrote in an answer that also sounds a contemporary note, is not whether "the Marines should be allowed to recruit on campus, but whether a University and its community, so devoted to the freedom of individuals to pursue their own chosen lifestyles and to speak freely, has the right or obligation to determine who may speak on campus or what may be said.

"To fulfill an immediate end," Gorsuch added, "we are likely to forget the underlying principle that every human being, according to our nation's proclamations, and reinforced by our University's standards, has an inalienable right to express himself or herself—whether we agree or not. Free speech works; it works better than any form of censorship or suppression; and in exercising [it] vigorously, the truth is bound to emerge." Thus, instead of a civil rights issue, Gorsuch turned the question into one involving free speech.

In 2017, at the time of his nomination, many reporters went back to these student writings, hoping to find in these collegiate tea leaves predictors of how, if confirmed, he might vote on the big issues of the day.

On February 1, the *Washington Post*'s Amy Wang wrote, "Gorsuch would write an occasional column for the paper called 'Fed Up.'

Although he had once seemed to express support for Cuban refugees rallying against Fidel Castro, in his later columns, Gorsuch rarely hid a disdain for campus activists, often using quotation marks when describing progressives or progressive issues.

"[H]e criticized protesters," Wang continued, "who had tried to block the eviction of a tenant from her university-owned apartment. 'Our protestors, it seems, have a monopoly on righteousness,' Gorsuch wrote in April 1988."

According to Amy Wang, Levitt quoted Gorsuch as saying, "I'm not sure that conservatism and Columbia can be easily connected. . . . However, the debate has been opened up considerably, and this is good. . . . Columbia is a better place than it was ten years ago. While conservatism may not be the dominant campus belief, it's healthy to have the mix that currently exists."

ALTHOUGH FEW OTHER PUBLICATIONS picked up on these student writings—or ran similar articles—in mid-March 2017, Arianna Huffington's *Daily Beast* ran a story by Brandy Zadrozny that took Neil Gorsuch to task for his support of and affection for his college fraternity:

> According to school newspaper reports and interviews with former Columbia students, FIJI's [the fraternity's nickname] reputation was unrivaled among Columbia's 12 other fraternities at the time—defined by accusations of hard-partying, racism, sexism, and date rape. FIJI, as one former member claimed, was known as a house where the spiked punch flowed, and party tents known as "smut huts" were erected for one clear purpose. . . .

In a spring 1988 farewell to graduating columnists, *Daily Spectator* editors handed out nicknames like "amazin' artiste," "drawing demon," and "fantastic feminist" to departing seniors. For Gorsuch, editors offered: "Neil Gorsuch, Fiji ain't all that bad."

When asked just what the nickname was meant to convey, Andrea Miller, a self-described "deeply involved campus activist" and former *Spectator* opinion-page editor who ran Gorsuch's columns, says she remembers it as a nod to his passionate and constant support of Phi Gamma Delta.

Brandy Zadrozny reached Michael Behringer, a member and one-time president of FIJI. According to her article, he told her, "any rumors of the fraternity's alleged impropriety are unfounded."

Behringer acknowledges the existence of gossip, mostly involving hard partying and allegations of sexism. "But there wasn't any evidence of [sexism or date-rape]," he says. "The thinking from some of these people was, 'You are a frat, therefore you must be a misogynist,' but there were never any real accusations made against us. There was just no substance behind it."

As Behringer notes, there is no public record of any woman accusing any member of the FIJI fraternity with rape or sexual misconduct before or during Gorsuch's time on campus. . . .

"There certainly were some members who were rowdier than others, but Neil wasn't part of that. He graduated in three years and spent his time focused on his studies and writing," Behringer says.

In the first week of February 2017, the Associated Press quoted several former colleagues on the start-up *Federalist Paper* who felt "co-founder Gorsuch was a thoughtful, unseasonably mature student dedicated to fostering debate on campus. 'He was not an ideologue,' says M. Adel Aslani-Far, a former writer and editor for the paper. 'At his core was that things should be thought through and presented and argued, not in a confrontational sense, but in the lawyer-judge sense.'"

The AP article continued:

Even during bleary-eyed, wee-hours sessions of squeezing an issue into print, Gorsuch made sure any cuts to "pro" and "con" commentaries didn't chop either argument unequally, said Aslani-Far, now a corporate lawyer. . . .

Even Gorsuch's political adversaries from Columbia recall him as civil and genteel. . . . And they can't forget how he sneered at campus activism, [writing that] protests over issues that included student elections, punishment for blockading buildings and a fraternity system under scrutiny over its treatment of women and black students "inspire no one and offer no fresh ideas or important notions."

Inspire no one? "Racial justice and freedom of speech and sexual assault and misogynistic behavior at frats, those were burning issues, and they remain burning issues to this day," says Andrea Miller, a former opinion-page editor at the *Columbia Daily Spectator*, who published Gorsuch's columns. . . . She's now president of the National Institute of Reproductive Health.

The Associated Press article concluded: "Overall, Gorsuch was 'someone who encouraged the floating of ideas for discussion,' willing to play devil's advocate to spur conversation, said one of the writers and editors for the *Federalist Paper*, Eric Prager, now a corporate attorney. "He describes the Fed as centrist. But to former campus activist-turned-civil-rights-lawyer Jordan Kushner of Minneapolis, Gorsuch was anything but. 'He's good at sounding reasonable, but . . . he took really right-wing positions' on protesters and the Iran-Contra affair, says Kushner, who tangled with Gorsuch on various issues."

Near the end of her long article, Zadrozny, the *Daily Beast* reporter, wrote, "As a Columbia undergraduate, Gorsuch was also keenly aware of the stamp his college years would leave on his future ambitions. '[Students] are coming to the realization that one's actions in college and one's conduct as a young adult will be examined in relentless detail should one [choose] to enter the public sector,' then junior Gorsuch and his colleagues presciently wrote in a November 1987 editorial in *The Federalist Paper*. 'One bare fact cannot be ignored. College students are to be held responsible for their actions to a certain degree.'"

GORSUCH, WHO FINISHED COLLEGE in three years instead of four, used his limited writing time to good effect, covering a variety of subjects.

On Ronald Reagan's foreign policy: "We need to clarify our policy-making, act with confidence, and decide: will we truly support the liberation of Nicaragua or will we try the 'hands-off' approach? To futilely condemn more Contras to death, as we did the Cuban freedom fighters at the Bay of Pigs and our own countrymen in Vietnam, to continue in ambivalent, contradictory policy-making, is no longer an acceptable alternative. It is time to step out of the mire of indecision that has frustrated American foreign policy over the last 20 years and that continues today."

On diversity: "But on at least one significant count, Columbia falls considerably short. Amazingly, radically different people from radically different backgrounds and locales share an incredible hegemony here on Morningside Heights in their radical politics. Truth is: Columbia does have a moral responsibility. It has a moral responsibility to overcome the tyrannical atmosphere of 'ideas' that has so dominated life on Morningside for the last 20 years; it has a responsibility to make the political, philosophical, and ethical experience here as diverse and varied as the cultural and ethnic experience."

On the movement to make Columbia's fraternities coed: "Drawing analogies to slavery and segregation, supporters of the coed rule say that Columbia has a moral obligation to recognize that changing our Greek system is a matter of equal rights. . . . What such heavy-handed moralism misses is the fact that Columbia is a pluralistic university, that its fraternity system is equally pluralistic, with options available for everyone. There is no one at Columbia who cannot join a fraternity or initiate a new one if they wish to do so."

On student protests: "With their 'issues,' campus 'progressives' have tried to convince us that we have an obligation to act. They insist that they are being harassed by 'terroristic fascists.' But what they forget to tell us is that they are asking for special treatment, acting as a vigilante squad while avoiding the weight of their own actions."

FROM 1988 TO 2006, the year he became a judge, Neil Gorsuch's writings were typical of each period: In law school he occasionally wrote papers for class assignments; while in private practice he wrote legal briefs and the kinds of communications that busy litigators write, such as memos and letters to keep clients informed of the latest developments in their cases, not to mention pleadings and other legal documents; and at the Department of Justice his writings were, for the most part, in response to requests for legal reasoning or information, still much like a lawyer-client relationship.

But once Gorsuch became a judge, he slipped easily into his old mode of rhetorical explicator. It had long been his belief that lawyers—and especially judges—should avoid legal jargon and formulaic phrasing and write so that the average intelligent person—not other judges and lawyers—could understand them. Also, he thought that the occasional well-turned phrase or bit of humor added to the making of an easily understood opinion. He made these his guiding principles, and it wasn't long before people—and not just lawyers—were noticing, commenting on, and enjoying his written opinions.

The following are among those writings frequently quoted:

We're beginning to think we have an inkling of Sisyphus's fate. Courts of law exist to resolve disputes so that both sides might move on with their lives. Yet here we are, forty years in, issuing our seventh opinion in the Ute line and still addressing the same arguments we have addressed so many times before. (*Ute Indian Tribe of the Unitah and Ouray Reservation, Plaintiff-Appellant* v. *Myton*, a municipal corporation)

Can you win damages in a defamation suit for being called a *member* of the Aryan Brotherhood prison gang on cable television when, as it happens, you have merely conspired with the Brotherhood in a criminal enterprise? The answer is no. While the statement may cause you a world of trouble, while it may not be precisely true, it is substantially true. And that is enough to call an end to this litigation as a matter of law. (*Bustos* v. *A & E Television Network*)

Haunted houses may be full of ghosts, goblins, and guillotines, but it's their more prosaic features that pose the real danger. Tyler Hodges found that out when an evening shift working the ticket booth ended with him plummeting down an elevator shaft. But as these things go, this case no longer involves Mr. Hodges. Years ago he recovered from his injuries, received a settlement, and moved on. This lingering specter of a lawsuit concerns only two insurance companies and who must foot the bill. And at the end of it all, we find, there is no escape for either of them. (*Western World Ins. Co.* v. *Markel Am. Ins. Co.*)

If a seventh grader starts trading fake burps for laughs in gym class, what's a teacher to do? Order extra laps? Detention? A trip to the principal's office? Maybe. But then again, maybe that's too old school. Maybe today you call a police officer. And maybe today the officer decides that, instead of just escorting the now compliant thirteen year old to the principal's office, an arrest would be a better idea. So out come the handcuffs and off goes the child to juvenile detention. My colleagues suggest the law permits exactly this option and they offer ninety-four pages explaining why they think that's so. Respectfully, I remain unpersuaded. (*A.M.* v. *Holmes*)

Often enough the law can be "a ass—a idiot" . . . and there is little we judges can do about it, for it is (or should be) emphatically our job to apply, not rewrite, the law enacted by the people's representatives. Indeed, a judge who likes every result he reaches is very likely a bad judge, reaching for results he prefers rather than those the law compels. So it is I admire my colleagues today, for no doubt they reach a result they dislike but believe the law demands—and in that I see the best of our profession and much to admire. It's only that, in this particular case, I don't believe the law happens to be quite as much of a ass as they do. (*A.M.* v. *Holmes*)

Andrew Yellowbear will probably spend the rest of his life in prison. Time he must serve for murdering his daughter. With that much lying behind and still before him, Mr. Yellowbear has found sustenance in his faith. No one doubts the sincerity of his religious beliefs or that they are the reason he seeks access to his prison's sweat lodge—a house of prayer and meditation the prison has supplied for those who share his Native American religious tradition. Yet the prison refuses to open the doors of that sweat lodge to Mr. Yellowbear alone, and so we have this litigation. While those convicted of crime in our society lawfully forfeit a great many civil liberties, Congress has (repeatedly) instructed that the sincere exercise of religion should not be among them—at least in the absence of a compelling reason. (*Yellowbear* v. *Lampert*)

In 2014, the quarterly legal publication *Green Bag*, which celebrates "Exemplary Legal Writing," gave an award to Judge Gorsuch for his opinion in the Yellowbear case.

The following are two more of Gorsuch's openings:

The Hatch Valley may be to chiles what the Napa Valley is to grapes. Whether it's the soil, the desert's dry heat, or the waters of the Rio Grande, the little town of Hatch, New Mexico, and its surroundings produce some of the world's finest chile peppers. Just ask any of the 30,000 people who descend on the place every year for the chile festival.

When you own property in the West you don't always own everything from the surface to the center of the Earth. Someone else may own the minerals lying underground and the right to access them. Someone else still might own the right to use the water flowing through your property. All this can invite confusion—and litigation. Ours is such a case, a battle between ranchers and miners over property claims they trace back to separate government grants an age ago.

GORSUCH'S WRITING ABILITY IS also evident in many of his speeches, in particular his tribute to Justice Scalia, his model for judicial philosophy. Entitled "Of Lions and Bears, Judges and Legislators, and the Legacy of Justice Scalia," it was delivered on April 7, 2016, at Cleveland's Case Western Reserve law school. It began:

> Since Professor Adler extended his invitation, the legal world suffered a shock with the loss of Justice Scalia. A few weeks ago, I was taking a breather in the middle of a ski run with little on my mind but the next mogul field when my phone rang with the news. I immediately lost what breath I had left, and I am not embarrassed to admit that I couldn't see the rest of the way down the mountain for the tears. From that moment it seemed clear to me there was no way I could give a speech about the law at this time without reference to that news.
>
> So tonight I want to say something about Justice Scalia's

legacy. Sometimes people are described as lions of their profession and I have difficulty understanding exactly what that's supposed to mean. Not so with Justice Scalia. He really was a lion of the law: docile in private life but a ferocious fighter when at work, with a roar that could echo for miles. Volumes rightly will be written about his contributions to American law, on the bench and off.

. . . I remember as if it were yesterday sitting in a law school audience like this one, listening to a newly minted Justice Scalia offer his Oliver Wendell Holmes lecture titled "The Rule of Law as a Law of Rules." He offered that particular salvo in his defense of the traditional view of judging and the law almost thirty years ago now. It all comes so quickly. But it was and remains, I think, a most worthy way to spend a life.

May he rest in peace.

IN HIS FIRST OPINION as a judge on the United States Supreme Court, *Henson* v. *Santander Consumer USA*, Neil Gorsuch showed that his few months away from writing legal prose had not dulled his pen. In the case, which involved interpreting the Fair Debt Collection Practices Act of 1977, he was writing for the unanimous majority. His opinion began in typical Gorsuch narrative style, and with an alliterative spin: "Disruptive dinnertime calls, downright deceit, and more besides drew Congress's eye to the debt collection industry."

Chapter Nine

NEIL GORSUCH: SCALIA LITE OR SCALIA 3.0?

For years, but especially since the day Neil Gorsuch was elevated to the highest court in the land, much has been made of his long-standing respect and admiration for the late justice Antonin Scalia. Clearly, Gorsuch liked the man personally, noting in his 2016 speech at Case Western Reserve law school that he cried when he got the news of Scalia's death. At the time of the Gorsuch nomination to the Supreme Court, one widely printed photo (taken by Gorsuch's brother, J.J.) showed Justice Scalia and Judge Gorsuch, arms over shoulders and both smiling broadly, on the shore of a river. Scalia had signed the photo, "Fond memories of a day on the Colorado, with warm regards." Gorsuch referred to that day when he said, in his opening statement to the Senate Judiciary Committee, "The Justice fished with the enthusiasm of a New Yorker. He thought the harder you slapped the line on the water, somehow the more the fish would love it."

In addition to the personal amity, Gorsuch absorbed and agreed with Scalia's approach to the law. Indeed, it can be said of originalism and textualism—with only a little exaggeration—that Scalia invented the combination, and Neil Gorsuch faithfully followed it.

In that same law school speech, Gorsuch also said:

But tonight I want to touch on a more thematic point and suggest that perhaps the great project of Justice Scalia's career

was to remind us of the differences between judges and legislators. To remind us those legislators may appeal to their own
moral convictions and to claims about social utility to reshape
the law as they think it should be in the future. But that
judges should do none of these things in a democratic society.
Judges should instead strive (if humanly and so imperfectly)
to apply the law as it is, focusing backward, not forward,
and looking to text, structure, and history to decide what a
reasonable reader at the time of the events in question would
have understood the law to be—not to decide cases based on
their own moral convictions or the policy consequences they
believe might serve society best.

As Justice Scalia put it, "[I]f you're going to be a good and
faithful judge, you have to resign yourself to the fact that
you're not always going to like the conclusions you reach. If
you like them all the time, you're probably doing something
wrong." It seems to me there can be little doubt about the
success of this great project. We live in an age when the job of
the federal judge is not so much to expound upon the common law as it is to interpret texts—whether constitutional,
statutory, regulatory, or contractual. And as Justice Kagan
acknowledged in her Scalia Lecture at Harvard Law School
last year, "we're all textualists now."

Capturing the spirit of law school back when she and I
attended, Justice Kagan went on to relate how professors
and students often used to approach reading a statute with
the question "[G]osh, what should this statute be," rather
than "[W]hat do the words on the paper say?" in the process
wholly conflating the role of the judge with the role of the

legislator. Happily, that much has changed, giving way to a return to a much more traditional view of the judicial function, one in which judges seek to interpret texts as reasonable affected parties might have done rather than rewrite texts to suit their own policy preferences.

And, as Justice Kagan said, "Justice Scalia had more to do with this [change] than anybody" because he "taught" (or really reminded) everybody how to do statutory interpretation differently.

ONE VERY CLEAR DIFFERENCE between the writing styles of Scalia and Gorsuch, two like-minded judges, is their tone. While Gorsuch is regularly and unfailingly polite, Scalia could be just the opposite.

In July 2015, a year before Scalia died, the well-known law professor and legal scholar and the dean of the Law School at UC Irvine, Erwin Chemerinsky, wrote a critical op-ed in the *Los Angeles Times* in which he said that Scalia's writing was setting "a terrible example for young lawyers," citing specifically his opinion in *Glossip* v. *Gross*, in which Justice Breyer had upheld the three-drug protocol used in lethal injection in the death penalty—"specifically whether it's a cruel and unusual punishment and thus in violation of the 8th Amendment. Scalia wrote a scathing response. He referred to Breyer's opinion as 'gobbledy-gook' and said his argument was 'nonsense.' He concluded by stating, 'Justice Breyer does not just reject the death penalty, he rejects the Enlightenment.'"

Chemerinsky considered this phrasing too harsh, asking, "What did Breyer do to deserve this treatment?" Former O'Connor clerk David Kravitz asked, "But why is a Scalia zinger entertaining?" And then answered, "It's entertaining because it shocks. It's entertaining because you cannot quite believe that a Supreme Court justice would treat one of his colleagues with such profound disrespect."

That phrase, "treat one of his colleagues with such profound disrespect," neatly delineates the essential difference between the approaches of Antonin ("Nino") Scalia and Neil McGill Gorsuch. Gorsuch doesn't do disrespect to colleagues; Scalia, at times, seemed to revel in it.

What made Scalia's name-calling hard to believe was that in person he was as affable, polite, and charming as, well, Neil Gorsuch. The sincere friendship between Scalia and the liberal icon Ruth Bader Ginsburg was often noted. (Both were great opera lovers, and playwright Derrick Ward wrote a comic operetta about their sincere friendship.)

Nonlawyers who'd met him also had their favorite pro-Scalia stories. Paul Anthony, a longtime television and radio personality (ubiquitous on Washington's Channel 26, the PBS station), who met the late justice through the National Italian American Foundation, recalls that he and his wife attended a wine tasting at a friend's house. Justice Scalia and his wife, Maureen, were at the same table.

At one point, the rather overbearing sommelier walked around the room asking guests wine-related questions. When he came to Scalia, the man—who apparently did not know he was addressing a Supreme Court justice—stood behind him and said, "Sir, what is the proper temperature for serving sauvignon blanc?"

Without turning around, Scalia said, in his distinctive voice, "I don't answer questions, I *ask* them."

Chuck Conconi is another well-known Washington personality of Italian-American heritage who met Justice Scalia and remembers his brilliance and wit. "I was writing a column for the *Washington Post*, and Scalia, who knew that I had written a book with Toni House, then the Supreme Court's spokeswoman, asked her, 'Who is this Chuck Conconi?' When we finally happened to meet, at a black-tie function at the Metropolitan Club, he was quite charming, and funny, and obviously very, very bright. We discussed our Italian–American roots, and I mentioned that I had recently discovered there was a tiny town in Cuba called Conconi, at which he said, 'Then I shall always remember you as a small town in Cuba.'"

IN AN ARTICLE HEADED "Neil Gorsuch's conservatism is different from Antonin Scalia's," *The Economist* magazine, in its March 23, 2017, issue, referred to what it termed "his affinity for a family of legal theories . . . most interesting or most worrisome":

> Though Mr. Trump promotes his nominee as drawn from the mould [*sic*] of Antonin Scalia . . . he represents a stark departure from a central feature of Mr. Scalia's jurisprudence. Mr. Scalia saw the constitution as a "practical and pragmatic" charter of government that neither requires nor permits "philosophising." In a right-to-die case in 1990, he quipped that the nine justices were no better suited to make fine distinctions on the morality of life support than "nine people picked at random from the Kansas City telephone directory." By contrast, Mr. Gorsuch seems more ready to let his philo-sophical judgments out [, tapping] into a tradition that reaches back to Thomas Aquinas and Aristotle. . . . Judicial adventures in metaphysics were anathema to the man who spent three decades in the seat to which Mr. Gorsuch aspires. . . . Scalia would be ill at ease with Mr. Gorsuch's natural-law jurispru-

dence as well, even if its implications more closely match his conservative views.

The New York Times said Gorsuch was "an Echo of Scalia in Philosophy and Style," but the Associated Press's Nancy Benac wrote, in *The Boston Globe*:

> Somewhere between the Republican caricature of the next justice of the Supreme Court as a folksy family guy and the Democrats' demonization of him as a cold-hearted automaton, stands Neil Gorsuch. Largely unknown six months ago, Gorsuch has seen his life story, personality and professional career explored in excruciating detail since he was nominated by President Trump 10 weeks ago.
>
> The portrait that emerges is more nuanced than the extremes drawn by his supporters and critics. Gorsuch is widely regarded as a warm and collegial family man, boss and jurist, loyal to his employees, and kind to those of differing viewpoints. He also has been shown to be a judge who takes such a "rigidly neutral" approach to the law that it can lead to dispassionate rulings with sometimes brutal results.

THUS IT APPEARS THAT while Justice Neil Gorsuch has great admiration for, shares some of the same judicial attitudes of, and also writes in a sprightly fashion similar to that of Antonin Scalia, the two are sufficiently different that it would be wrong to say, or even to suggest, that the former is a clone of the latter.

Just as Justice Thomas has proven to be his own (very conservative) man—and not, as it was predicted at the time of his confirmation, a paler, less focused version of Scalia, so, too, will Neil Gorsuch, the judge who speaks for himself, prove to be his own, distinctive man.

Veteran National Public Radio legal correspondent Nina Totenberg wrote on July 1, 2017, the day after Neil Gorsuch's first Supreme Court opinions were handed down:

> It is unusual to see a new justice's ideological footprints so clearly in his first year or two on the high court. Indeed, most new justices, including those with long careers on the lower courts, are somewhat hesitant at first. They understand that the Supreme Court's word is the final word, and that looking at issues from this new perspective is somewhat different from the perspective of a lower court judge, whose job is to carry out the mandates of a higher court.
>
> But Justice Gorsuch seems both sure-footed and sure of himself and his views. Though he was confirmed in time to hear only the final two weeks of the term's oral arguments, his votes and opinions in those cases—and others that the court has disposed of since he was sworn in—paint a vivid picture of a justice on the far right of the current Supreme Court bench. Indeed, he voted 100 percent of the time with the court's most conservative member, Clarence Thomas, according to SCOTUSblog.
>
> If Thomas is Gorsuch's new best friend, in terms of votes, his second-best friend statistically is Justice Samuel Alito, with whom he voted next most often.

Were he somehow still here, Antonin Scalia would undoubtedly be pleased.

Chapter Ten

THE CONFIRMATION HEARINGS

In the days and weeks leading up to March 20, 2017, politicians, pundits, and the people voiced their opinions of both the nominee and the process. On Thursday, February 2, two days after Trump nominated Gorsuch, the *Washington Post* stated, in its lead editorial:

> President Trump's nomination of Judge Neil Gorsuch for the Supreme Court elicited an immediate, furious, and depressingly predictable reaction. Senate Minority Leader Charles E. Schumer (D-NY) called him an ideologue in a tweet sent a mere half hour after Mr. Trump made his announcement, and liberal senators such as Sherrod Brown (D-Ohio) and Elizabeth Warren (D-Mass) announced they would oppose the nomination not long after that. Conservative activist groups, meanwhile, vowed to go on an election-year-style campaign to advance Mr. Gorsuch's nomination. The politicization of the judiciary, in other words, continues apace.

Three of the four columns on that same day's op-ed page dealt with the Gorsuch nomination. On February 1, George F. Will took issue with a statement by Justice Scalia that there is no philosophizing in the Constitution, and expressed the hope that because he has a doctorate in philosophy and jurisprudence from Oxford, where he studied with John Finnis (who wrote *Natural Law and Natural Rights*), Gorsuch "will effect a philosophic correction." And, in a column headed "It's Time to make Republicans pay for their supreme hypocrisy," the liberal E. J. Dionne, Jr., opined that "We are in for a festival of GOP hypocrisy in the debate over [the Gorsuch nomination]." And, finally, in a side-by-side column, Republican senator Mitch McConnell, the architect of the Garland blockade, gave voice to that hypocrisy, stating that Scalia's seat on the highest court "does not belong to one president or one political party. It belongs to the American people."

On the same day Trump picked Gorsuch, the *New York Times*, as expected, editorialized against the nomination: "In normal times, Judge Gorsuch—a widely respected and, at 49, relatively young judge with a reliably conservative voting record—would be an obvious choice for a Republican president. These are not normal times."

On the day after Gorsuch was nominated, Alex Swoyer of the *Washington Times*, a conservative voice, wrote, in part: "Neil Gorsuch is a conservative judge and gifted writer who leaves no doubt where he stands, making him a natural successor to the late Justice Antonin Scalia, court watchers said Tuesday. . . . Several rulings where the judge acted to protect religious objectors to Obamacare's contraceptive mandate earned him praise from conservatives, who predicted he would be a trustworthy vote for them on the high court. And he was also seen as one of the more easily confirmable judges on the list Mr. Trump said he was choosing from."

Swoyer's *Times* colleague S. A. Miller wrote:

The pick immediately drew praise from conservatives, including an outpouring of support from Senate Republicans. "He's awesome. He's fantastic," said Sen. Mike Lee, a Republican

who was on Mr. Trump's list of prospective nominees for
the high court. . . . The nomination, however, also quickly
found detractors. Liberal groups raised alarms about his stance
on gun control, abortion and contraception, environmental
protection and the role of big money in politics. "His danger-
ous views favor polluters and industry over the rights of the
people," said Sierra Club Executive Director Michael Brune.
"We strongly urge senators, who are elected to represent and
protect the American people, to stand up for families across
the nation, oppose this nomination, and use every tool in the
shed to block this extremist nominee."

In the forty-seven days between the nomination and start of the
Senate Judiciary Committee hearings, both sides solidified their positions.

On February 10, Senate Minority Leader Charles Schumer
stepped into the fray with a *New York Times* article entitled "We
Won't Be Fooled Again." In it, he expressed his opinion that Chief
Justice John Roberts had not kept his promise, made in *his* confirmation hearing, to be impartial. Roberts had said he himself would
simply be an umpire and would call "balls and strikes." Instead, according to the senator, he became "a tenth player," putting the Court
clearly in the conservative camp. Schumer wrote that Judge Gorsuch
gave off a similar vibe. "My fellow senators should know that Judge
Gorsuch was eerily similar to Judge Roberts. He played the part but
was entirely unwilling to engage in a substantive discussion that—
crucially—could have given me confidence in his independence as
a judge. Judge Gorsuch must be far more specific in his answers to
straightforward questions about his judicial philosophy and opinions
on previous cases."

As Senator Schumer pointed out, the nominee categorically refused to answer those questions, which came as no surprise to citizens, whether or not they are attorneys, who follow Supreme Court nominations.

★

TRADITIONALLY, THE NOMINEE IS accompanied—the word commonly used is "shepherded"—by a team of same-party individuals led (usually) by a former senator who is known and respected by the senators the nominee will visit, even those of the opposite party. In the case of Neil Gorsuch, the guide (or "shepherd") was former senator Kelly Ayotte, the moderate Republican from New Hampshire, who narrowly lost her bid for reelection in 2016.

This was an "unlikely selection by Trump," reported the *Washington Post*, because "she spoke out against his candidacy and was seen as having been on a blacklist for appointments to the new administration." Ayotte headed a seven-member team of Republican operatives with both senatorial and White House experience.

In the almost seventy meetings Gorsuch had with senators, he received praise from Democrats as well as fellow Republicans, though no member of the opposite party came forward as a result of those meetings to say he or she would vote in favor of the Gorsuch nomination. This is important because Gorsuch needed eight Democrats to join the Senate's fifty-two Republicans in order to reach the magic number of sixty votes that would put him on the high court.

But if this did not happen, if he didn't get eight defectors from the Democratic line—and few analysts thought he would—the Republicans, who controlled the Senate and the Judiciary Committee, could adopt what is called "the nuclear option" and change the rules so that it would take a simple majority (not a supermajority of sixty) to move a nominee for the Supreme Court from the Judiciary Committee to the full Senate for a vote.

In 2013, then–Senate Majority Leader Harry Reid of Nevada changed the Senate rule that had been in place for forty years so that all presidential nominees *except* for those for the Supreme Court could be approved by a simple majority. He reflected, in a *New York Times* op-ed article, "We changed the Senate rules to guarantee a president's nominees a simple-majority vote. . . . I doubt any of us envisioned Donald J. Trump's becoming the first president to take office under the new rules. But what was fair for President Obama is fair for President Trump."

A FUNNY THING HAPPENED on the way to the hearings. On several occasions in the first month of his presidency, Donald Trump had attacked, on Twitter, federal judges who had ruled against him or one of his policies, such as the Muslim travel ban, referring to them as "so-called judges." On February 9, 2017, a day after he had met with Judge Gorsuch in his Senate office, Connecticut Democrat Richard Blumenthal told reporters that when he asked the judge about Trump's comments, Gorsuch had called them "disheartening" and "demoralizing." This, of course, was considered major news—a Supreme Court nominee criticizing the president who had nominated him.

Trump's reaction was to go after Blumenthal. He tweeted, "Sen. Richard Blumenthal, who never fought in Vietnam when he said for years he had (major lie), now misrepresents what Judge Gorsuch told him?"

PolitiFact reported that "Gorsuch has not responded to Blumenthal publicly himself. However, Republican strategist Ron Bonjean, who is assisting the White House on the Gorsuch nomination, confirmed Blumenthal's account to reporters. Later, other senators said Gorsuch made similar statements in their private meetings, including Sen. Ben Sasse, R–Neb, and Senate Minority Leader Chuck Schumer, D–N.Y. . . . Former Sen. Kelly Ayotte, R–N.H., who is assisting Gorsuch in his Capitol Hill meetings, had a slightly different take. She said in a statement to NBC that Gorsuch said *any* attack on the judiciary is 'disheartening' and 'demoralizing'—speaking generally rather than responding directly to Trump's recent comments: 'Judge Gorsuch has made it very clear in all of his discussions with senators, including Sen. Blumenthal, that he could not comment on any specific cases and that judicial ethics prevent him from commenting on political matters,' Ayotte's statement said. 'He has also emphasized the importance of an independent judiciary, and while he made clear that he was not referring to any specific case, he said that he finds any criticism of a judge's integrity and independence disheartening and demoralizing.'"

The *PolitiFact* article concluded, "Again, we can't know for sure exactly what Gorsuch said in his private meetings with Blumenthal and others. It's possible that Gorsuch responded to Trump's comments directly, but it's also possible he was asked about Trump's comments and then attempted to respond more generally. But a spokesman for Gorsuch confirmed Blumenthal's account, and several senators said Gorsuch told them that he found Trump's comments about the judiciary 'disheartening' and 'demoralizing.' Overall, the evidence seems to point away from Trump's claim that Blumenthal 'misrepresents' his conversation with Gorsuch."

★

By 9:00 a.m. on Monday, March 20, 2017, the doors to the public entrance of SH 216, Senate Hart (building) 216—the huge hearing room the Senate Judiciary Committee had chosen as the site of its hearings on the nomination of Neil Gorsuch to the United States Supreme Court—were open, and all was in readiness for the hearing.

According to the Senate Historical Office, "The newest of the Senate office buildings is named for Michigan senator Philip A. Hart (1912–1976). In his 18-year Senate career, Hart distinguished himself as a man of deep personal conviction and integrity and a steadfast advocate for the common man, [which] earned him the moniker, 'The Conscience of the Senate.'"

The Hart Senate Office Building opened in 1982, becoming the only congressional office building named after a sitting (or living) member. Both the room and building have had their moments in recent American history. In 2013, the confirmation hearings for Massachusetts Democratic senator John Kerry to become secretary of state were held in SH 216, as were the 2009 hearings for Sonia Sotomayor to join the Supreme Court. And in 2001, the Capitol Police announced the discovery of anthrax in a freight elevator in the Hart Building, which was then closed for a week of decontamination.

From both before and after its opening, the building had fans and detractors. The massive structure—its nine aboveground stories contain a million square feet of internal space, one-third of which is usable space—is covered in white marble from Vermont, with the floor of the atrium Tennessee marble. The centerpiece of the atrium is a huge Alexander Calder structure called *Mountains and Clouds*, which consists of a mobile made of aluminum plates (the clouds) and a fifty-five-foot-high stabile painted matte black (the mountain). The contrast between the black of the stabile and the white Vermont marble on the surrounding walls is most dramatic.

One of the Hart Building's fiercest critics was the late senator Daniel Patrick Moynihan (D–NY). Dismayed by both its look and its price tag, in May 1981 he introduced a satirical Sense of the Senate resolution that read: "Whereas in the fall of 1980 the frame of the new Senate Office Building was covered with plastic sheathing in order that construction might continue during winter months; and Whereas the plastic cover has now been removed revealing, as feared, a building whose banality is exceeded only by its expense; and Whereas even in a democracy there are things it is well the people do not know about their government: Now, therefore, be it resolved, that it is the sense of the Senate that the plastic cover be put back."

Moynihan's criticism aside, three decades after its opening, the Hart Senate Office Building is a well-received, if not necessarily well-loved, part of the Capitol grounds.

THE LAST TIME NEIL Gorsuch faced Senate confirmation—in 2005, when President George W. Bush nominated him to be a judge on the Court of Appeals for the Tenth Circuit—he was approved by a unanimous voice vote. Nothing even remotely close to that was expected to happen this time. The stakes were too different, and the political climate was, in a word, ugly.

Like all its predecessors, the Gorsuch hearings began with statements. First, the committee chair and the ranking minority member would read their opening statements, and then the remaining eighteen individual members (ten Republicans and eight Democrats) of the Judiciary Committee would read theirs. Committee chairman

Chuck Grassley (R-IA) had said the hearings would take three or four days.

Court watchers and other interested parties had a good idea of what was to come. When the new president nominated Gorsuch, Senator Elizabeth Warren (D-MA) reacted almost viscerally. In a speech on the Senate floor, in addition to "disastrous," she called the president's nomination "a threat to our American values."

A very different view of the same man appears in the bipartisan letter sent on Tuesday, February 14—Valentine's Day—to Senators Grassley and Feinstein, the ranking Republican and Democrat on the committee. Signed by thirty-nine of Judge Gorsuch's former clerks not currently clerking for a justice, it stated, "Our political views span the spectrum, and among us you will find differing views on how the Senate handled the nomination of Judge Merrick Garland," they wrote, "but we are united in our view that Judge Gorsuch is an extraordinary judge. All of us strongly support his confirmation as the next Associate Justice of the Supreme Court." The former clerks said he had the ability to transcend partisan politics and honor both the Constitution and the rule of law with "tremendous care and discipline."

Touching on a personal level, the clerks wrote, "Most importantly, we know Judge Gorsuch to be a man of decency and integrity. In his work life, he treats everyone around him with the utmost respect—staff, interns, students, clerks and his colleagues on the bench. But we also know something of his life outside of chambers, as a man utterly devoted to his wife and two teenage daughters. That is because Judge Gorsuch welcomes his clerks into his extended family. For most of us, Denver is far from family and friends. Judge Gorsuch made us feel at home for our year there in countless ways—from inviting us to his home to share a meal together to hosting hikes and ski trips in the

Colorado mountains. And after we left his chambers, he has continued to teach and mentor us, never hesitating to give us his time and sound guidance." The former law clerks ended the letter by calling Gorsuch "a remarkable judge and a remarkable man," and they urged the Senate to move on his nomination at once.

★

ON THE FIRST DAY of the hearings, SH 216 was more than a match for the crowd that had been approved (by the Judiciary Committee) to attend the hearings. The room is the size of a football field with the main door in one "end zone," and the committee members at the other. The nominee sits at a table directly in front of the committee, facing the chairman and ranking minority member, and the committee members sit, according to party and by seniority, on a long, slightly curved dais. The two-story room is topped by television-quality lights built into the ceiling, and on each side of the room there are rectangular booths (a lower and an upper one) where television crews can report without impeding the views of ground-floor reporters. Four very-large-screen television sets—two on each side—provide spectators with an unobstructed view of the proceedings.

Immediately behind the witness table are three rows of chairs, ten to a row, with an aisle in the middle, for members of Congress and the witnesses' friends and family members. For this hearing, the nominee's entourage all but filled that section. Beyond the rows of chairs is a large space filled with long tables for the media (with electrical outlets on the floor beneath the tables), each of which can sit twenty people. Behind this bull pen section is another set of chairs for guests, all of whom had to have been cleared for attendance by the Judiciary Committee staff.

★

THE FIRST STATEMENT WAS that of the Judiciary chairman, Charles Grassley (R–IA), followed by that of the ranking minority member, Dianne Feinstein (D–CA) Both legislators are eighty-three, and neither one is a lawyer, a lack that apparently does not bother them or hinder their ability to question judicial nominees. Senator Grassley is on record as having said that while he might see more "nuances" if he were an attorney, he feels comfortable basing his questions and comments on his background as a farmer.

In her twenty years on the Judiciary Committee, Senator Feinstein has never voted for a Republican nominee, but Grassley, who has been on the committee since his election in 1982, voted to approve both Stephen Breyer and Ruth Bader Ginsburg.

In his statement, Grassley welcomed Gorsuch, heaped praise on him for his record and accomplishments, and then said:

> To this senator, what's far more distressing about each Executive overreach and each failure to defend the law, is the damage it does to our constitutional order. The damage those abuses inflict is far more difficult to undo than the policies that animated them. For as John Adams observed, "Liberty, once lost, is lost forever." So, the separation of powers is just as critical today as it was during the last administration. And the preservation of our constitutional order—including the separation of powers—is just as crucial to our liberty today as it was when our founding charter was adopted. . . .
>
> So if you hear that you're *for* some business or *against* some plaintiff—don't worry. You've heard all of that stuff before. It's an old claim, from an even older playbook. You and I and the American people know whose responsibility it is to cor-

rect a law that produces a result that you dislike. It's the men and women sitting here with me.

Good judges understand this. They know it isn't their job to fix the law. In a democracy, that right belongs to the people.

It's for this reason that Justice Scalia said, "If you're going to be a good and faithful judge, you have to resign yourself to the fact that you're not always going to like the conclusions you reach. If you like them all the time, you're probably doing something wrong."

Judge, I look forward to hearing more about your exceptional record. And I look forward to the conversation we'll all have about the meaning of our Constitution and the job of a Supreme Court Justice in our constitutional scheme.

Next came the ranking minority member of the Judiciary Committee, Dianne Feinstein. She, too, praised the nominee, but got right to the point with her concerns.

Judge Gorsuch, I want to welcome you and your family. . . . President Trump repeatedly promised to appoint someone "in the mold of Justice Scalia" and said that the nomination of Judge Gorsuch illustrates he's "a man of his word."

For those of us on this side, our job today is not to theoretically evaluate this or that legal doctrine or to review Judge Gorsuch's record in a vacuum. Our job is to determine whether Judge Gorsuch is a reasonable, mainstream conservative or is he not.

★

CHAIRMAN GRASSLEY THEN ANNOUNCED that each senator on the committee would have ten minutes to question the nominee and thirty minutes the next day, and urged them to keep on the clock.

For the next three and a half hours, the senators went at it. The Republicans praised the western judge to the eastern skies. Utah's Mike Lee (who had been one of the twenty-one judges on President Trump's list of potential Supreme Court nominees and had argued cases before the Tenth Circuit) sounded younger than his age when he said Gorsuch was "awesome" and "fantastic." Orrin Hatch's praise was notably over the top, and Lindsey Graham of South Carolina got a few chuckles from the audience when he admitted he was not exactly the president's favorite Republican senator.

The Democrats on the committee, especially Dick Durbin of Illinois, wasted little time with niceties but got right to the crux of their objections. Durbin accused Gorsuch of being "part of a Republican strategy to capture our judicial branch of government at every level. That is why the Senate Republicans kept this Supreme Court seat vacant for more than a year and why they left 30 judicial nominees who had received bipartisan approval of this committee to die on the Senate calendar as President Obama left office." Durbin then added, "Despite all of this, you are entitled to be judged on your merits."

The Illinois Democrat made reference to two cases that greatly bothered those who opposed the Gorsuch nomination, the Hobby Lobby case previously discussed and TransAm trucking. In the latter case, a driver, Alphonse Maddin, was driving a trailer through Illinois in winter when the brakes on the trailer froze. Gorsuch's Tenth Circuit fellow judges found in favor of the truck driver, whom TransAm had dismissed, but Gorsuch dissented, writing:

[A] trucker was stranded on the side of the road, late at night, in cold weather, and his trailer brakes were stuck. He called his company for help and someone there gave him two options. He could drag the trailer carrying the company's goods to its destination (an illegal and maybe sarcastically offered option). Or he could sit and wait for help to arrive (a legal if unpleasant option). The trucker chose None of the Above, deciding instead to unhook the trailer and drive his truck to a gas station. In response, his employer, TransAm, fired him for disobeying orders and abandoning its trailer and goods. It might be fair to ask whether TransAm's decision was a wise or kind one. But it's not our job to answer questions like that. Our only task is to decide whether the decision was an illegal one.

CNN's legal analyst Paul Callan opined:

Under the rules of the US Department of Labor, a truck driver can't be fired for refusing to "operate" his vehicle because of "safety concerns." But in his dissent, Gorsuch didn't buy the argument that a refusal to "operate" the vehicle was even involved. In fact, he "operated" his truck, driving it to a gas station against company orders that he should have remained with the trailer.

Callan said Gorsuch

was demonstrating his firm belief in the principle that the actual words of a law should be strictly applied by the court. This doctrine, often referred to as textualism, stands for the proposition that it is up to the legislature to make [the laws]. Gorsuch maintained that the actual words of the statute in question would only back the driver when he was "operating" both the cab and the trailer as a single unit. Obviously, he couldn't "operate" the truck and trailer together and drive away for help and warmth because the brakes on the trailer were frozen. The other judges on the 10th Circuit were willing to apply a dollop of common sense and give the driver the benefit of the doubt.

Conservatives such as Gorsuch abhor this vision of the law because they believe it robs the democratically elected legislature of the right to make law in accordance with the will of the electorate. Instead liberal judges "create" their own law with each new case, creating uncertainty about how future judges will handle future cases.

The twin brother of textualism in constitutional law is the doctrine of originalism, which holds that when interpreting the Constitution, a judge should stay as close to the "original intent" of the Founding Fathers as possible. But even true believers in originalism have to bend to the reality of changing times on occasion. After all, the 13 original states often used punishments such as whippings and displaying criminals in stocks and pillories until the mid-19th century. Today even most originalists would find such punishments to be "cruel and unusual" violations of the US Constitution.

Paul Callan ended his CNN article with a bit of advice: "Gorsuch would be wise to remember the oft-quoted words of Scalia, 'I'm an originalist and a textualist, not a nut.' Even Scalia probably would have let the truck driver thaw out at the gas station."

Senator Durbin got in a good parting shot when he said, in a harsh tone, that the weather on that day was "not as cold as your dissent." He ended his questioning by stating, "[This president is] going to keep you busy."

Gorsuch appeared to take this criticism in stride, but during Durbin's questioning, his jaw was set a bit more firmly, and there was a noticeable furrow in his brow. Louise, the judge's wife, who is also able to maintain a fixed, almost stern visage, had a grim look on her pleasant face.

DEMOCRATIC SENATOR FROM RHODE Island Sheldon Whitehouse was impressive in his give-and-take with the nominee regarding dark money (that which cannot be traced back to its giver) and the role it plays in modern-day politics. He told Gorsuch that it is very hard to find the names of the people who contributed to the conservative group Judicial Watch, which has said it is spending $1 million to get Gorsuch confirmed.

"Hypothetically," Whitehouse continued, "it could be your friend Mr. Anschutz [the Colorado billionaire who has been a Gorsuch client and then mentor for several decades]. We don't know because it is dark money."

He then asked Gorsuch why someone thought it was worth $1 million to get him confirmed.

"You'd have to ask them," Gorsuch responded, and Whitehouse countered, "I can't, because I don't know who they are. It's just a front group."

An interesting take on the frozen trucker case was provided by the legal blog *Above the Law*, which surveyed a group of Al Maddin's fellow truck drivers to see what they made of the controversy. Surprisingly, they were not particularly sympathetic.

According to *Above the Law* editor Elie Mystal, who wrote the story, "[The truckers'] legal reasoning sounds close to a 'contributory negligence' standard. For their perspective, if Maddin put himself in a position to run out of gas, then he caused the events that led to his own firing."

ANOTHER SENATOR UPSET BY Gorsuch's ruling in the trucker case was Al Franken (D-MN), the former writer and performer on *Saturday Night Live*. Franken made no bones about his view of the facts in the frozen trucker case—and Judge Gorsuch's dissent. He pushed and pushed at Gorsuch to tell him what he would do if he found himself in the same dilemma. Gorsuch said, "I don't know what I would have done if I were in his shoes. I don't blame him at all for doing what he did do. I thought a lot about this case. I totally empathize."

"I would have done exactly what he did," Franken immediately replied, and Gorsuch, sounding almost on the verge of sarcasm, countered with, "Yeah, I understand that."

The junior senator from Minnesota rolled right on:

I think everybody here would have done exactly what he did.
And I think that's an easy answer, frankly. I don't know why
you had difficulty answering that. Okay, so you decided to
write a thing in dissent. If you read your dissent, you don't
say it was like subzero; you say it was cold out. The facts that
you describe in your dissent are very minimal. . . . You go to
the language of the law. And you talk about that. . . . And you

decided they had the right to fire him, even though this law says you may not fire an employee who refuses to operate a vehicle, because he did operate the vehicle.

By this point, the questioning had become repetitive, and Gorsuch, perhaps in an attempt to speed things up, said, "That's the gist of it."

Franken concluded with a statement that made almost all media accounts of the dialogue: "When using the plain meaning rule would create an absurd result, courts should depart from the plain meaning. It is absurd to say this company is in its rights to fire him because he made the choice of possibly dying from freezing to death or causing other people to die possibly by driving an unsafe vehicle. That's absurd. Now I had a career in identifying absurdity, and I know it when I see it. And it makes me—you know, it makes me question your judgment."

Franken ended his time by mentioning that both White House senior advisor Steve Bannon and Chief of Staff Reince Priebus had included Gorsuch in what they referred to as their plan to "deconstruct the administrative state" and roll back forty years of regulatory law.

Senator Franken then asked the nominee, "Are you comfortable with your nomination being described in such transactional terms?" Gorsuch quickly replied, "There is a lot about this process that makes me uncomfortable."

AT FIFTEEN MINUTES BEFORE 3:00 p.m., the nominee was finally formally introduced—by Senate tradition, the nominee is "introduced" by a senator or senators from his or her home state and, sometimes, also by others—to the committee and, via CSPAN, the country and world, by three men, two of whom were Democrats.

It is traditional for the senators from the nominee's home state to introduce him or her. In this case, it was Republican Cory Gardner and Michael Bennet, a Democrat. Said the latter, "I'm not here to take a position or persuade any of our colleagues how to vote. I am keeping an open mind about this nomination and expect this week's hearings will shed light on Judge Gorsuch's judicial approach and views of the law."

Throughout the first day of the hearings, the name Merrick Garland seemed to come up as often as the nominee's. Bennet was no exception, saying that the way the Senate treated Garland was "an embarrassment to this body," and adding, "it is tempting to deny Judge Gorsuch a fair hearing . . . but two wrongs do not make a right."

The second Democratic "presenter" was Neal Katyal, President Barack Obama's acting solicitor general, with whom Gorsuch had served on the Federal Appellate Rules Committee. Katyal told the Judiciary Committee, "It is a tragedy of national proportions that Merrick Garland is not on the court. And it would take a lot to get over that," but added, "Indeed, there are less than a handful of people that the president could have nominated to even start to rebuild that loss of trust . . . But in my opinion Neil Gorsuch is one."

Earlier, in an op-ed article, Katyal had written, "I am hard-pressed to think of one thing President Trump has done right in the last 11 days since his inauguration," and called Garland "perhaps the most qualified nominee ever for the high court," but he said, as quoted by *Politico*, "Gorsuch . . . should be at the top of the list. I believe this, even though we come from different sides of the political spectrum. . . . I have seen him up close and in action [and] he brings a sense of fairness and decency to the job, and a temperament that suits the nation's highest court."

Some liberals immediately dissed Katyal's support of Gorsuch. Nan Aron, president of Alliance for Justice, told CNN, "The elite legal class has closed ranks around Gorsuch and this is just the latest example. It seems as if too many of them are too impressed by Gorsuch's personal polish and resume to see past them to how damaging his record is when it comes to the impact on everyday people." This theme would be echoed and expanded upon in the remaining days of the hearings.

Shortly after three, Neil Gorsuch addressed the members of the Judiciary Committee: "Mr. Chairman, Senator Feinstein, Members of the Committee: I am honored and I am humbled to be here. Since coming to Washington, I have met with over 70 senators. You have offered a warm welcome and wise advice. Thank you. I also want to thank the President and Vice President. They and their teams have been very gracious to me and I thank them for this honor. I want to thank Senators Bennet and Gardner and [Solicitor] General Katyal for their introductions. Reminding us that—long before we are Republicans or Democrats—we are Americans. Sitting here I am acutely aware of my own imperfections. But I pledge to each of you and to the American people that, if confirmed, I will do all my powers permit to be a faithful servant of the Constitution and laws of our great nation."

The nominee went on to thank, in order, his wife and children, his parents and grandparents, several other relatives, "my fellow judges across the country," and his legal mentors (especially Justices White and Scalia), and closed by describing what it had meant to him, over the past decade, to be a judge. (For a complete version of Judge Gorsuch's statement, see Appendix A.)

★

ON TUESDAY AND WEDNESDAY, the twenty-second and twenty-third of March, the Judiciary Committee members went at it long and hard—long on both sides of the aisle and hard on the Democratic side. With the questioners alternating between Republicans (the majority, because the Senate is controlled by that party) and Democrats, the tone and content changed from gushing praise to acidic denunciation with the speed of a badminton bird.

When Senator Patrick Leahy (D-VT) asked Gorsuch if he thought the president had the power to authorize torture if it violated the law, the nominee, sounding like the law professor he has been, quickly listed torture-banning precedents and then, when the senator repeated the question, declared, "No man is above the law," an answer that gave hope to those who feared that Gorsuch, once on the Court, would do only what Trump and the hard right wanted.

Another exchange that seemed to imply his independence from the man who had nominated him occurred when Lindsey Graham (R-SC) asked him what he would do if the president asked him to vote to overturn *Roe* v. *Wade*. Gorsuch, in a voice that was both louder and firmer than usual, replied, "Senator, I would have walked out the door." ("At that," CNN reported later that day, "the room fell silent.") But Gorsuch wasn't finished with his answer, adding, "That's not what judges do. They don't do it at that end of Pennsylvania Avenue, and they shouldn't do it at this end either."

When Patrick Leahy asked him if a blanket religious test would be consistent with the Constitution, the man hoping to become the 113th justice of the U.S. Supreme Court replied, "We have a constitution and it does guarantee free exercise. It also guarantees equal protection of the laws. And a whole lot else. The Supreme Court . . . said that due process rights extend even to undocumented persons in this country. I will apply the law. I will apply the law faithfully and fearlessly. Anyone, any law is going to get a fair and square deal with me."

Chairman Grassley then wondered if Gorsuch would have trouble ruling against Donald Trump, who twice during the campaign had criticized judges who'd ruled against him, labeling them "so-called judges." Gorsuch replied, "That's a softball [question], Mr. Chairman. I have no difficulty ruling against or for any party . . . based on what the law and the facts in the particular case require."

As for the Democrats' concern, voiced by ranking minority member Dianne Feinstein, that he favored corporations, i.e., the big guy, over workers, the little guy, Judge Gorsuch said, "I'd like to convey to you, from the bottom of my heart, that I am a fair judge. . . . I have participated in 2,700 opinions over ten and a half years, and if you want cases where I've ruled for the little guy as well as the big guy, there are plenty of them."

Time and again, Democratic senators tried to get the nominee to say how he would rule on certain types of cases in the future, and time and again Gorsuch would refuse, causing one senator to remark that he had "set a new standard for evasiveness." But, in fact, the nominee was only following the example set in 1993 by the liberal heroine Ruth Bader Ginsburg (aka "The Notorious RBG"), who'd famously said, as noted earlier, that she would give "no hints, no forecasts, no previews." Nonetheless, the Democratic senators—who had to be well aware that no matter how many times it was rephrased, he was not going to answer that type of question—persisted, apparently in the belief that they were making Gorsuch look bad.

By the middle of day three of the hearings, the proceedings began to resemble Japanese Noh theater, the slow-moving classical plays that can last as long as eight hours. Gorsuch managed at all times to keep his composure and showed few signs of the frustration he must have felt at being dragged over the same ground again and again.

From time to time that pent-up frustration resulted in a quotable line, as when, at the end of day two, which ran for ten straight hours, Rhode Island Democrat Sheldon Whitehouse kept at Gorsuch over the *Citizens United* case (which held that corporations could give money to political campaigns without having to disclose the identity of their donors). Later, Senator Mike Lee (R–UT), calling it "unfair" for Whitehouse to belabor Gorsuch with questions about *Citizens United*–related issues, asked the nominee if he'd had any involvement in the Supreme Court ruling.

"I was not involved," Gorsuch said, and then added, forcefully, "Nobody speaks for me. Nobody. I am a judge. I don't have spokesmen. I speak for myself."

WITH THE NOMINEE NOT present, the fourth and final day of the hearings was given over to expert witnesses, both pro and con. The for-Gorsuch experts had, by and large, been invited by the Republicans on the committee, and the antis—mainly representatives of women's and environmental groups—had asked to be heard or had been invited by the Democrats. Their statements and positions generally echoed those of the Republicans and Democrats on the committee.

When Mitch McConnell realized that Minority Leader Chuck Schumer (D–NY) was serious about filibustering to delay the full Senate's vote on Gorsuch (Republicans wanted him on the Court as soon as possible so that he could, and they believed would, cast the deciding conservative vote on several cases believed to be deadlocked four to four), the Majority Leader announced he would use what is termed the "nuclear option"—dropping the requirement for approval of the nomination from sixty to fifty votes (plus the vice president's)—and that is what he did.

Senator Joe Manchin, the West Virginia Democrat who had voted for Gorsuch but opposed changing the rules, told the *Washington Post*, using a rather archaic metaphor, that "George Washington had it right when he called the Senate 'the saucer'—We're the saucer—should be anyway. Should be cooling off that tea. . . . The hot tea's going to scald you now. It's going to burn you."

Senator Susan Collins (R–ME), a critic of the nuclear option, said the fault lies in what the Senate has become: "There's such a profound lack of trust, and that's what many of us are committed to trying to rebuild. We need to make very clear to the leaders on both sides that there's no support for curtailing our existing ability to filibuster legislation."

Her leader in the Senate, Mitch McConnell, agreed with Senator Collins about the need to preserve the legislative filibuster, but had his own idea of who was to blame for his having deployed the nuclear option—the Democrats. In a Sunday, April 9, op-ed page article in the *Washington Post*, he wrote:

> The day after Neil Gorsuch's nomination to the Supreme Court was announced, I wrote about his sterling credentials, record of independence and long history of bipartisan support—and predicted they would matter little to hard-left special interests that invariably oppose the Supreme Court nominees of any Republican president. I asked Democrats to ignore those extreme voices and their attacks and join us instead in giving Gorsuch fair consideration and an up-or-down

vote, as we did for the first-term Supreme Court nominees of Presidents Bill Clinton and Barack Obama.

Unfortunately, Democrats made a different choice. . . .

On Thursday, Democrats mounted the first successful partisan filibuster of a Supreme Court nominee in U.S. history; in other words, a partisan Democratic minority tried to block the bipartisan majority that supported Gorsuch from even voting on his nomination. It was a direct attack on the traditions of the Senate and yet another extreme escalation in Democrats' decades-long drive to transform judicial confirmations from constructive debates over qualifications into raw ideological struggles.

Their success in tearing down Robert Bork in 1987 taught Democrats that any method was acceptable so long as it advanced their aim of securing power. In 2003, when President George W. Bush was nominating judges, Democrats pioneered the idea of using routine filibusters to stop them; in 2013, when Obama was nominating judges, Democrats invoked the "nuclear option" to prevent others from doing the same. It was a tacit admission that they should have respected the Senate's long-standing tradition of up-or-down votes for judicial nominees in the first place.

The Majority Leader closed with this thought: "I ask Democrats to consider the significant things we've been able to achieve in recent years when we worked together. Democrats can continue listening to those on the left who call for blind 'resistance' to anything and everything this president proposes, but we can get more done by working together. Perhaps this is the moment Democrats will begin again to listen to the many Americans—the people who sent us here—who want real solutions, so we can work together to help move our country forward."

ON FRIDAY, APRIL 7, by a vote of fifty-four to forty-five, the U.S. Senate confirmed Neil Gorsuch as the 113th justice of the Supreme Court. The Republicans had tried to get him confirmed under the old sixty-yes-vote rule, but when that failed they, led by McConnell, methodically moved to change the rules so that all that was needed for the nominee to be confirmed was a simple majority. The next vote made Neil Gorsuch a member of the United States Supreme Court.

THE CONFIRMATION PROCESS FEATURED two unusual displays of physicality. The first came when Senator McConnell came off the Senate floor. Flush with victory, he awkwardly high-fived several fellow Republican colleagues, in a manner that made it obvious he is not comfortable with the gesture.

The second display occurred the following Monday immediately after the swearing-in in the Rose Garden of the White House. After having been sworn in by Justice Anthony Kennedy, once his boss and mentor and now his fellow justice, Neil Gorsuch, now officially a Supreme, stepped forward and put his arms around and hugged Anthony Kennedy. While being hugged, Justice Kennedy, apparently surprised by Gorsuch's impulsive gesture, kept his arms at his side and did not return the hug.

IN THAT ROSE GARDEN ceremony, the proud president said, "I got it done in the first 100 days . . . you think that's easy?" Press Secretary Sean Spicer followed suit, proclaiming: "As we hit day 81 in the President's administration, we have done so many great things, including nominate and confirm a Supreme Court justice, roll back more regulations than any president in modern times, roll back the Obama-era war on coal, oil and natural gas, restore confidence in the economy. . . . We're now seeing historic levels of consumer, CEO, homebuilder, manufacturer confidence. There's been a 12% gain on the stock market. And we've even seen a real resurgence in the mining industry."

The *New York Times* agreed, at least in part:

> The moment was a triumph for President Trump, whose campaign appeal to reluctant Republicans last year rested in large part on his pledge to appoint another committed conservative to succeed Justice Antonin Scalia, who died in February 2016. However rocky the first months of his administration may have been, Mr. Trump now has a lasting legacy: Judge Gorsuch, 49, could serve on the court for 30 years or more.
>
> "As a deep believer in the rule of law, Judge Gorsuch will serve the American people with distinction as he continues to faithfully and vigorously defend our Constitution," the president said. . . . The confirmation was also a vindication of the bare-knuckled strategy of Senate Republicans, who refused even to consider President Barack Obama's Supreme Court pick, Judge Merrick B. Garland, saying the choice of the next justice should belong to the next president.

The *Times* editorial continued: "The bruising confrontation has left the Senate a changed place. Friday's vote was possible only after

the Senate discarded longstanding rules meant to ensure mature de-
liberation and bipartisan cooperation in considering Supreme Court
nominees."

Several days later, Linda Greenhouse, the *Times'* widely respected
legal correspondent, wrote a column entitled "The Broken Supreme
Court," in which she said that by changing the rules, the Republicans
had jeopardized the Court:

> It was raw politics all the way down, without even a fig leaf
> of a nonpolitical rationale. I'm not naïve. All presidents yearn
> for a Supreme Court legacy, and many tell fibs about the
> nominees they choose. President Reagan presented Robert
> H. Bork as a "moderate." He wasn't. President George H. W.
> Bush described Clarence Thomas as the best-qualified per-
> son for the job. He wasn't. That's all just part of the game.
> Of course the Supreme Court nomination and confirmation
> process is political; how could it be otherwise?
>
> But the Republicans rewrote the rules well before their
> decision last week to abolish the filibuster for Supreme Court
> confirmation votes. Making an existing Supreme Court
> vacancy a highly visible part of an electoral strategy stamps
> the court as an electoral prize, pure and simple. In doing so, it
> places the court in a position of real institutional peril.

CONSERVATIVE REPUBLICANS WERE EAGER for Gorsuch to join the
Court and start hearing—and voting on—cases, including several
that had already been argued, with no decision rendered, and brand-
new cases that the Court will take up at the end of the 2016–17 term.
The subjects of these cases include a California case that will test the

state's restrictions on carrying a concealed gun in public, a religious rights versus gay rights case, and one involving funding limits for church schools.

The first two of those three cases may or may not be heard in this term, as they are unscheduled, but the third, the Trinity (Missouri) Lutheran case, was heard on Wednesday, April 19, Gorsuch's third day on the Court. The dispute in the case arose when Trinity Lutheran Church, which operates a preschool, applied to the state of Missouri for a grant to rubberize (using material from old tires) the surface of its playground and was turned down because the state's constitution bars giving money "directly or indirectly, in aid of any church, sect, or denomination of religion." Claiming the state's denial constituted an unconstitutional burden on its free exercise of religion, the church sued.

Conservatives hoped that Gorsuch's dissenting vote as an appellate court judge in the Hobby Lobby case (he was in favor of giving a religious exemption to a Christian family business that had refused to pay for insurance that provided contraceptives for its employees) meant he would rule for the church in the Trinity Lutheran case. The justices kept the lawyers on their feet for more than an hour of intense questioning, but Gorsuch himself was quiet, in contrast to his first day as a justice, two days earlier.

Justice Sonia Sotomayor commented, "I'm not sure it's a 'free exercise' [of religion] question. No one is asking the church to change its beliefs. The state is just saying it doesn't want to be involved in giving [public] money to the church." But her colleague Elena Kagan said, "You're denying one set of actors from competing [for the grant money] because of religion," which, she said, is a "clear burden on a constitutional right."

And Justice Stephen Breyer, generally considered a liberal, wanted to know, "[D]oes the Constitution of the United States permit a state or a city to say, 'We give everybody in this city police protection, but not churches? We give everybody fire protection, but let churches burn down?'" Because Gorsuch asked the state's lawyer just a few brief questions, there was no hint as to how he might rule, thus thwarting any predictions based on his vote in the Hobby Lobby case. There was a touch of the surreal—or, to borrow Senator Franken's word, "absurd"—about the whole proceedings because, as *SCOTUSblog* reported, "Moreover, the justices seemed inclined to go ahead and decide the case even though Missouri had announced last week that it had changed the policy at issue in the case to allow churches to compete for the grants in the future." Apparently the fact that twenty-three other states have laws on their books similar to the Missouri ban was a factor in the Court's decision to go ahead with arguments in the Trinity Lutheran case. According to *SCOTUSblog*, "The end result could be an important ruling on the disbursement of funds by state and local governments to religious institutions."

Conclusion

When, on April 7, 2017, Neil McGill Gorsuch was confirmed as a member of the United States Supreme Court, the forty-nine-year-old jurist became a very distinguished person in the eyes of the outside world. Not so inside the Court itself, which has seen dozens of its members come and go over the years. To them, Neil Gorsuch was a newbie, a rookie, and was treated as such.

The newest justice has to take notes during private Court conferences (if there are no clerks or court assistants around) and must speak last when they discuss how they plan to vote after they've heard oral arguments. This doesn't sound all that demeaning, but the neophytes' duties don't end there.

One task sounds like the high court version of KP. As Elena Kagan told Neil Gorsuch and his fellow appellate judge Tim Tymkovich at an event in Colorado, "I've been on the cafeteria committee for six years. Steve Breyer was on the cafeteria committee for 13 years. I think this is a way to kind of humble people. You've just been confirmed to the United States Supreme Court. And now you're going to monthly cafeteria committee meetings where literally the agenda is 'What happened to the good recipe for chocolate chip cookies?'"

Kagan reportedly contributed to a frozen yogurt machine in the cafeteria after she was confirmed in 2010—she also had to go fix a colleague's soup if it was "too salty." Another thing, and this is the most important junior justice responsibility, is, "I open the door," Kagan said. "Literally, if I'm like in the middle of a sentence—let's say it's my turn to speak or something—and there's a knock on the door, everybody will just stare at me, waiting for me to open the door. It's like a form of hazing. [Chief Justice John Roberts told a judicial conference in 2011 that cafeteria duty is meant to bring new justices "back down to earth after the excitement of confirmation and appointment."] So that's what I do, I open the door. Pronto."

IN *HENSON* v. *SANTANDER Consumer USA*, his first opinion as a justice on the United States Supreme Court, Neil Gorsuch wrote:

> From that scrutiny emerged the Fair Debt Collection Practices Act, a statute that authorizes private lawsuits and weighty fines designed to deter wayward collection practices. So perhaps it comes as little surprise that we now face a question about who exactly qualifies as a "debt collector" subject to the Act's rigors. Everyone agrees that the term embraces the repo man—someone hired by a creditor to collect an outstanding debt. But what if you purchase a debt and then try to collect it for yourself—does that make you a "debt collector" too? That's the nub of the dispute now before us. . . .
>
> After all, is it really impossible to imagine that reasonable legislators might contend both ways on the question whether defaulted debt purchasers should be treated more like loan originators than independent debt collection agen-

cies? About whether other existing incentives (in the form of common law duties, other statutory and regulatory obligations, economic incentives, or otherwise) suffice to deter debt purchasers from engaging in certain undesirable collection activities? . . . After all, it's hardly unknown for new business models to emerge in response to regulation, and for regulation in turn to address new business models. Constant competition between constable and quarry, regulator and regulated, can come as no surprise in our changing world. But neither should the proper role of the judiciary in that process—to apply, not amend, the work of the People's representatives.

The judgment of the Court of Appeals is Affirmed.

Court watchers gave Neil Gorsuch high marks for his maiden effort. John O. McGinniss, a professor of constitutional law at Northwestern, wrote in *City Journal*, to which he is a contributing editor: "Neil Gorsuch has spent only a fraction of a term as a Supreme Court justice, but few justices have had a more promising start. He has shown himself a careful textualist in reading statutes, a serious originalist in interpreting the Constitution, and an adherent of judicial restraint—and he has done all this with an engaging style that will allow him to reach over the heads of Court watchers and critics to the people. He seems an ideal schoolmaster for the American republic— a jurist whose every opinion is a lucid primer on the civics of our governance."

David Savage of the *Los Angeles Times* and Robert Barnes of the *Washington Post*, two veteran legal reporters, both wrote articles on Gorsuch's first opinion. In an article headed "In his first Supreme Court Opinion, Gorsuch shows writing flair, strict interpretation of law," Savage wrote, "Justice Neil M. Gorsuch used his first high court opinion Monday to write a concise, pointed essay on how the justices should decide cases—by following the 'plain terms' of the law, not by updating an old statute to meet new problems. 'These are matters for Congress, not this court,' he wrote."

And Barnes's piece began, "Justice Neil M. Gorsuch got a cushy assignment for his first Supreme Court opinion—a unanimous ruling affirming a lower court—and used it to showcase both his writing style and much-touted devotion to a textual interpretation of the laws Congress passes."

The written record of the Gorsuch era on the U.S. Supreme Court had begun.

★

BACK IN DECEMBER 2016, before Gorsuch was even nominated, University of Denver law professor Justin Marceau, who has litigated civil rights and death penalty cases, told the *Denver Post* that Neil Gorsuch was "'a predictably socially conservative judge who tends to favor state power over federal power.'"

According to the *Post*, "That kind of deference, Marceau adds, can create a difficult obstacle for civil rights cases, which often try to reel in 'rogue' state laws.

"So what impact would Gorsuch have on the Supreme Court?

"'It means that we would see a judge who, while perhaps not as combative in personal style as Justice Scalia, is perhaps his intellectual equal,' said Marceau, 'and almost certainly his equal on conservative jurisprudential approaches to criminal justice and social justice issues that are bound to keep coming up in the country.'"

"Whatever the topic of his opinions, Gorsuch has developed a reputation for language that is both sharp and conversational within a captivating narrative style—one that might be judiciously spiced for maximum effect. 'Word on the street is that Judge Gorsuch has his law clerks add contractions to his opinions, to make himself sound more folksy—and therefore more appealing as a possible SCOTUS nominee.'"

★

ON MONDAY, APRIL 17, 2017, Neil M. Gorsuch, who is either the 113th or the 101st Supreme Court justice in U.S. history—media accounts used the first number; Chief Justice John Roberts, in welcoming Gorsuch to the Court, used the second—took the bench with his eight fellow justices to hear oral argument in three cases. When he entered and took the far right seat, where the newest, most junior justice always sits, he had a broad smile on his face.

NPR's longtime legal correspondent Nina Totenberg observed, "Despite his white hair, Gorsuch looked for all the world like a kid on his first day of high school, proud to be with the big guys, and sitting tall, with a tiny grin on his face."

Before the lawyers began their arguments in the first case, Chief Justice Roberts noted the occasion (but not the bitter confirmation battle that had preceded it) by saying, "[I]t gives me great pleasure on behalf of myself and my colleagues to welcome Justice Gorsuch as the 101st associate justice of this court," apparently subtracting the number who joined the court from outside as the chief justice (a short list that includes John Marshall). "Justice Gorsuch, we wish you a long and happy career in our common calling." To which the new justice replied, with obvious sincerity, "Thank you to each of my new colleagues for the very warm welcome I received this week. I appreciate it very much."

No one knew if Justice Gorsuch, on his rookie appearance at the high court plate, would be silent, as Clarence Thomas almost always is, or if he would emulate his hero, Justice Scalia, who seldom was. It did not take long to find out.

Over three hours of argument in three dry, legally technical cases, Gorsuch was an active, almost avid, questioner. Having skipped a judges' conference meeting the previous Thursday so he could bone up on the three cases scheduled to be heard on the following Monday, Justice Gorsuch must have pulled the SCOTUS equivalent of an all-nighter, for it was soon apparent that he had the details of each case down cold.

"He asked crisp and colloquial questions," the *New York Times* reported, "and he kept asking them if he did not find the lawyers' answers satisfactory."

The first case, which was about where to file Civil Service and discrimination cases, was, in the words of Justice Samuel Alito, "unbelievably complicated." He said, "Nobody who is not a lawyer and no ordinary lawyer could read these statutes and figure out what they are supposed to do." He then asked, "Who wrote this statute? Someone who takes pleasure in pulling wings off of flies?"

In apparent agreement, Justice Sotomayor got a laugh when she said to one of the lawyers, "If we go down your route, and I'm writing that opinion—which I hope I'm not . . ." At that Gorsuch smiled, probably realizing that if the decision was in the majority then he, as the newest justice, might well receive that assignment from his chief.

Gorsuch stayed silent for all of ten minutes, and then unleashed a string of questions, six in all. Reported the *New York Times*:

But Justice Gorsuch approached the case with relish, and he made what is likely to become one of his signature points, that the court's job is limited to reading the words of the statute under review.

"Looking at the plain words of the statute," he told a lawyer, Christopher Landau. "If you could just help me with that."

Justice Gorsuch grew a little self-conscious as he kept pressing. "I'm sorry for taking up so much time," he said. "I apologize."

Later, when Mr. Landau started reading the statutory text aloud, Justice Gorsuch said: "Keep going. Keep going."

As the lawyer and the justice examined the language together, Mr. Landau, in a tone of pleased surprise, said, "I think I am maybe emphatically agreeing with you."

Justice Gorsuch welcomed the comment. "I hope so," he said, to laughter.

Mr. Landau said his client was "not asking the court to break any new ground" by interpreting the statute to allow some filings.

Justice Gorsuch agreed, in a way. "No," he said, "just to continue to make things up."

In *Perry* v. *Merit Systems Protection Board*, Justice Gorsuch asked a signature question: "Wouldn't it be a lot easier if we just followed the plain text of the statute? What am I missing?"

Mr. Fletcher, a lawyer for the federal government, said there were reasons to interpret the statute broadly. But Gorsuch persisted: "Not reasons," he said. "Where in the language?"

In the second case, Gorsuch sounded a bit peckish when he said to another lawyer, "If you would just answer my question, I would be grateful." When the lawyer tried, Gorsuch relaxed the pressure: "I'll let you go."

In an article titled "Neil Gorsuch Sounded a Lot Like Justice Scalia on His First Day on the Job," the *Huffington Post* concluded, "Overall, the rookie justice was poised, respectful and unafraid to leave a mark on his first day. By one empiricist's count, he spoke more words than six other justices. (According to attorney blogger Adam Feldman, only Roberts and Kagan talked more.) He also seemed friendly with Justice Sonia Sotomayor, who sits directly to his right and with whom he'll be spending lots of time on the bench—at least until the next vacancy occurs."

It was the first of what will most likely be many more days on the Supreme Court for Neil M. Gorsuch—and the first of what will surely be many more questions.

ON SEPTEMBER 26, TWO weeks before the Supreme Court was to begin its 2017 term, Gorsuch appeared not once but twice and gave speeches that some critics equated with campaigning for Senator Mitch McConnell. Again, Gorsuch made news for doing something that indicated he fully intended to be his own man. And, also once again, his actions stoked controversy. This was the second time since the Court had adjourned in May that he had made headlines for doing something his critics saw as partisan. The first was when he accepted an invitation from the Fund for American Studies, a conservative group, to give the main talk at its Defending Freedom Luncheon on September 29, 2017. The main objection to this event was that it was being held at Trump International Hotel.

According to the *New York Times*, "Some experts in legal ethics and many liberal groups questioned the wisdom and prudence of Justice Gorsuch's decision to speak at the hotel. Several lawsuits are challenging the constitutionality of foreign payments to companies controlled by President Trump." Critics also protested the justice's joint appearance with McConnell, but supporters quickly pointed out that liberal judges like Ruth Bader Ginsberg have often spoken to liberal groups. Perhaps this appearance would not have raised voices as much as it did had Neil Gorsuch not stated, as he did so emphatically at his confirmation hearings: "There is no such thing as a Republican judge or Democratic judge. We just have judges."

The *Washington Post*'s Supreme Court reporter, Robert Barnes—in a September 27, 2017, article titled "Gorsuch speeches raise questions of independence, critics say"—quoted Stanford law professor Deborah L. Rhode, whom he described as a "highly cited authority on legal ethics": 'All of this indicates he's just ethically tone-deaf.'" And in *Above the Law*, Kathryn Rubino, an editor there, put the matter in the form of an implied prediction: "If you're a liberal, Gorsuch 'glad-handing' for the GOP probably only registers about a 3 on the outrage meter. . . . But, you don't have to be skilled at reading tea leaves to see this as a bad omen for the likely tenor of Judge Gorsuch's jurisprudence."

Whatever may turn out to be the case, one thing has become quite clear: Supreme Court Associate Justice Neil Gorsuch, like Antonin Scalia, the man he replaced, will say what he wants to say ("I am a judge. I speak for myself."). The tone may be different, but the tune will be the same. It wasn't an accident that in his formative years, he made Scalia his personal hero. As Robert Barnes poined out at the end of his September 27 article, "[Gorsuch] . . . told his audiences that he has moved into Scalia's old chambers and even taken possession of the huge stuffed elk head, 'Leroy,' that dominated one wall. 'The truth is I am delighted to share space with Leroy because it turns out we share quite a lot in common,' Gorsuch said. 'We're both native Coloradans. We both received a rather shocking summons to Washington, D.C. [And] neither of us is ever going to forget Justice Scalia.'"

Author's Note

O ne day in mid-August of 1984, I got a call from Flip Brophy, then an agent in the office of Sterling Lord Literistic (and now for many years its president). She said the agency had a new client who needed a writer, and asked if I'd be willing to meet with Anne Gorsuch Burford, who had resigned, under pressure, as head of the Environmental Protection Agency (EPA) the previous year.

Knowing only what I'd gotten from media accounts, I hesitated. Flip said, "Just go meet her and let me know what you think." I did, and called Flip back with a positive report: "She's just like my sister: She's very bright, very Republican, and very nice. I'd be happy to work with her." And so we did, and in 1986 McGraw-Hill published *Are You Tough Enough?* by Anne Burford with John Greenya.

Although qualified to do so, Anne rarely bragged about herself, but occasionally about her three children. Because the oldest, high school junior Neil (his younger brother and sister were still in primary school), was already giving evidence of a bright future, he was the one she talked about most often.

When the book came out, Anne thanked me in the acknowledgments section and also thanked my friend Mary Ellen Lynch (now Mary Ellen George), the secretary to the businessman from whom I rented my office. Anne would come in, tape a portion of the book with me, and then try to entice Mary Ellen into joining her at Sam and Harry's down the street, saying. "Okay, he'll be tied up for at least an hour; let's go get a drink." Mary Ellen said recently, "I was just a little secretary, but she was so down-to-earth and such great fun that I'd go—as long as my boss was out of town."

That was the right word for Anne—fun. And humorous. She once told a group of newspaper reporters, "My father always said, if you have something difficult to do you should do it right away. So the first thing I do every morning is read the *Washington Post*."

When Neil was ready for college, and then, just three years later, law school, I remember her mixture of pride and dismay that he would be going to not one but two "elite eastern liberal schools." Apparently, Neil, who'd had no trouble competing academically at Columbia and had won scholarships for both college and law school, (plus his PhD from Oxford), felt otherwise.

Anne moved back home to Denver, we kept in touch, and we often had lunch on her trips back to the nation's capital. However, after 2000, I saw less and less of Anne, though I did hear she'd started using a portable oxygen device, so I wasn't greatly surprised when I picked up the *Washington Post* on Thursday, July 22, 2004, and read that she had died of cancer.

Sometime in the late 1990s, I got a call from John Daniel, Anne's former chief of staff, inviting me to lunch with him and Neil Gorsuch. I found Neil, then a practicing lawyer in Washington, to be friendly, obviously bright (like both his parents), down-to-earth, and clearly not stuck on himself. That was the only time we met, but in 2006 when he was named to the court of appeals I received an invitation to his investiture ceremony in Denver. Lacking a crystal ball, I did not go; now, of course, I wish I had.

When I read he was being considered as Justice Scalia's replacement, I began the process that led to the writing of this book. In 2017, I requested an interview with him. But he declined, just as he'd done with all press requests for interviews since becoming a federal judge in 2006.

In writing this book, I feel as if I have come full circle: the book is *about* Neil, but it is also *for* his mother.

Appendix A

NEIL GORSUCH'S (MARCH 21, 2017) STATEMENT
BEFORE THE SENATE JUDICIARY COMMITTEE

I could not even attempt this without Louise, my wife of more than twenty years. The sacrifices she has made and her giving heart leave me in awe. I love you so much. We started off in a place very different from this one: a small apartment and little to show for it. When Louise's mother first came to visit, she was concerned by the conditions. As I headed out the door to work, I will never forget her whispering to her daughter—in a voice just loud enough for me to hear—Are you sure he's really a lawyer?

To my teenage daughters watching out West. Bathing chickens for the county fair. Devising ways to keep our determined pet goat out of the garden. Building a semi-functional plyboard hovercraft for science fair. Driving eight hours through a Wyoming snowstorm with high school debaters in the back arguing the whole way. These are just a few of my favorite memories. I love you impossibly.

To my extended family across Colorado. When we gather, it's dozens of us. We hold different political and religious views, but we are united in love. Between the family pranks and the pack of children running rampant, whoever is hosting is usually left with at least one drywall repair.

To my parents and grandparents. They are no longer with us, but there's no question on whose shoulders I stand. My mom was one of the first women graduates of the University of Colorado law school. As the first female assistant district attorney in Denver, she helped start a program to pursue deadbeat dads. And her idea of day care sometimes meant I got to spend the day wandering the halls or tagging behind police officers. She taught me that headlines are fleeting—courage lasts.

My dad taught me that success in life has little to do with success. Kindness, he showed me, is the great virtue. He showed me too that there are few places closer to God than walking in the wilderness or wading a trout stream. Even if it is an awfully long drive home with the family dog after he encounters a skunk.

To my grandparents. As a boy, I could ride my bike to their homes and they were huge influences. My mom's father, poor and Irish, started working to help support his family as a boy after losing his own dad. But the nuns made sure he got an education, and he became a doctor. Even after he passed away, I heard from grateful patients who recalled him kneeling by their bedsides to pray together. His wife, my grandmother, grew up in a Nebraska home where an icebox wasn't something you plugged into the wall but something you lowered into the ground. With seven children, she never stopped moving—or loving.

My dad's father made his way through college working on Denver's trolley cars. He practiced law through the Great Depression. And taught me that lawyers exist to help people with their problems, not the other way around. His wife came from a family of pioneers. She loved to fish. And she taught me how to tie a fly.

I want to thank my friends. Liberals and conservatives and independents, from every kind of background and belief, many hundreds have written this committee on my behalf. They have been there for me always. Not least when we recently lost my uncle Jack, a hero of mine and a lifelong Episcopal priest. He gave the benediction when I took my oath as a judge eleven years ago. I confess I was hoping he might offer a similar prayer for me this year. As it is, I know he is smiling.

I want to thank my fellow judges across the country. Judging is sometimes a lonely and hard job. But I have seen how these men and women work with courage and collegiality, independence and integrity. Their work helps make the promises of our constitution and laws real for us all.

I want to thank my legal heroes. Justice White, my mentor. A product of the West, he modeled for me judicial courage. He followed the law wherever it took him without fear or favor to anyone. War hero. Rhodes scholar. And, yes, highest-paid NFL football player of his day. In Colorado today there is God and John Elway and Peyton Manning. In my childhood it was God and Byron White.

I also had the great fortune to clerk for Justice Kennedy. He showed me that judges can disagree without being disagreeable. That everyone who comes to court deserves respect. And that a legal case isn't just some number or a name but a life story.

Justice Scalia was a mentor too. He reminded us that words matter—that the judge's job is to follow the words that are in the law—not replace them with words that aren't. His colleagues cherished his great humor too. Now, we didn't agree about everything. . . . The Justice fished with the enthusiasm of a New Yorker. He thought the harder you slapped the line on the water, somehow the more the fish would love it.

Finally, there is Justice Jackson. He wrote clearly so everyone could understand his decisions. He never hid behind legal jargon. And while he was a famously fierce advocate for his clients as a lawyer, he reminded us that, when you become a judge, you fiercely defend only one client—the law.

By their example, these judges taught me about the rule of law and the importance of an independent judiciary, how hard our forebears worked to win these things, how easy they are to lose, and how every generation must either take its turn carrying the baton or watch it fall.

Mr. Chairman, these days we sometimes hear judges cynically described as politicians in robes. Seeking to enforce their own politics rather than striving to apply the law impartially. But I just don't think that's what a life in the law is about. As a lawyer working for many years in the trial court trenches, I saw judges and juries—while human and imperfect—trying hard every day to decide fairly the cases I presented.

As a judge now for more than a decade, I have watched my colleagues spend long days worrying over cases. Sometimes the answers we reach aren't ones we would personally prefer. Sometimes the answers follow us home and keep us up at night. But the answers we reach are always the ones we believe the law requires. For all its imperfections, the rule of law in this nation truly is a wonder—and it is no wonder that it is the envy of the world.

Once in a while, of course, we judges do disagree. But our disagreements are never about politics—only the law's demands. Let me offer an example. The first case I wrote as a judge to reach the Supreme Court divided 5 to 4. The Court affirmed my judgment with the support of Justices Thomas and Sotomayor—while Justices Stevens and Scalia dissented. Now, that's a lineup some might think unusual. But actually it's exactly the sort of thing that happens—quietly, day in and day out—in the Supreme Court and in courts across our country. I wonder if people realize that Justices Thomas and Sotomayor agree about 60 percent of the time, or that Justices Scalia and Breyer agreed even more often than that. All in the toughest cases in our whole legal system.

Here's another example. Over the last decade, I've participated in over 2,700 appeals. Often these cases are hard too: only about 5 percent of all federal lawsuits make their way to decision in a court of appeals. I've served with judges appointed by President Obama all the way back to President Johnson. And in the Tenth Circuit we hear cases from six states—in two time zones—covering 20 percent of the continental United States. But in the West we listen to one another respectfully, we tolerate and cherish different points of view, and we seek consensus whenever we can. My law clerks tell me that 97 percent of the 2,700 cases I've decided were decided unanimously. And that I have been in the majority 99 percent of the time.

Of course, I make my share of mistakes. As my daughters never tire of reminding me, putting on a robe doesn't make me any smarter. I'll never forget my first day on the job. Carrying a pile of papers up steps to the bench, I tripped on my robe and everything just about went flying. But troublesome as it can be, the robe does mean something—and not just that I can hide coffee stains on my shirt. Putting on a robe reminds us that it's time to lose our egos and open our minds. It serves, too, as a reminder of the modest station we judges are meant to occupy in a democracy. In other countries, judges wear scarlet, silk, and ermine. Here, we judges buy our own plain black robes. And I can report that the standard choir outfit at the local uniform supply store is a pretty good deal. Ours is a judiciary of honest black polyester.

When I put on the robe, I am also reminded that under our constitution, it is for this body, the people's representatives, to make new laws. For the executive to ensure those laws are faithfully enforced. And for neutral and independent judges to apply the law in the people's disputes. If judges were just secret legislators, declaring not what the law is but what they would like it to be, the very idea of a government by the people and for the people would be at risk. And those who came to court would live in fear, never sure exactly what governs them except the judge's will. As Alexander Hamilton explained, "liberty can have nothing to fear from" judges who apply the law, but liberty "ha[s] everything to fear" if judges try to legislate too.

IN MY DECADE ON the bench, I have tried to treat all who come to court fairly and with respect. I have decided cases for Native Americans seeking to protect tribal lands, for class actions like one that ensured compensation for victims of nuclear waste pollution by corporations in Colorado. I have ruled for disabled students, prisoners, and workers alleging civil rights violations. Sometimes, I have ruled against such persons too. But my decisions have never reflected a judgment about the people before me—only my best judgment about the law and facts at issue in each particular case. For the truth is, a judge who likes every outcome he reaches is probably a pretty bad judge, stretching for the policy results he prefers rather than those the law compels.

As a student many years ago I found myself walking through the Old Granary burial ground in Boston, where Paul Revere, John Hancock, and many of our founders are buried. I came across the tombstone of a lawyer and judge who today is largely forgotten— as we are all destined to be soon enough. His name was Increase Sumner. Written on his tombstone over two hundred years ago was this description—"As a lawyer, he was faithful and able; as a judge, patient, impartial, and decisive; In private life, he was affectionate and mild; in public life, he was dignified and firm. Party feuds were allayed by the correctness of his conduct; calumny was silenced by the weight of his virtues; and rancor softened by the amenity of his manners."

These words stick with me. I keep them on my desk. They serve for me as a daily reminder of the law's integrity, that a useful life can be led in its service, of the hard work it takes, and an encouragement to good habits when I fail and falter. At the end of it all, I could hope for nothing more than to be described as he was. If confirmed, I pledge that I will do everything in my power to be that man.

Appendix B

Honorable Neil M. Gorsuch, *2016 Sumner Canary Memorial Lecture: Of Lions and Bears, Judges and Legislators, and the Legacy of Justice Scalia*, 66 Case W. Res. L. Rev. 905 (2016)
Available at: http://scholarlycommons.law.case.edu/caselrev/vol66/iss4/3

2016 Sumner Canary Memorial Lecture: Of Lions and Bears, Judges and Legislators, and the Legacy of Justice Scalia

Honorable Neil M. Gorsuch

Case Western Reserve Law Review·Volume 66·Issue 4·2016

Of Lions and Bears, Judges and Legislators, and the Legacy of Justice Scalia

Honorable Neil M. Gorsuch

I f you were looking for a talk tonight about the maddening maze of our civil justice system—its exuberant procedures that price so many out of court and force those in it to wade wearily through years and fortunes to win a judgment—you came to the right place. Almost.

When Professor Adler kindly asked me to share a few words with you tonight, that was my intended topic. I'd just finished penning opinions in two cases. One was older than my law clerks and had out-lived many of the plaintiffs. The other had bounced up and down the federal court system for so long it was nearly as ancient as Cleveland's championship drought. You know you're in trouble when the Roman numeral you use to distinguish your opinion from all the others of the same name draws closer to X than I. Needless to say, I was eager to talk about civil justice reform.

But that was then and this is now. Since Professor Adler extended his invitation, the legal world suffered a shock with the loss of Justice Scalia. A few weeks ago, I was taking a breather in the middle of a ski run with little on my mind but the next mogul field when my phone rang with the news. I immediately lost what breath I had left, and I am not embarrassed to admit that I couldn't see the rest of the way down the mountain for the tears. From that moment it seemed clear to me there was no way I could give a speech about the law at this time without reference to that news.

So tonight I want to say something about Justice Scalia's legacy. Sometimes people are described as lions of their profession and I have difficulty understanding exactly what that's supposed to mean. Not so with Justice Scalia. He really was a lion of the law: docile in private life but a ferocious fighter when at work, with a roar that could echo for miles. Volumes rightly will be written about his contributions to American law, on the bench and off. Indeed, I have a hard time thinking of another Justice who has penned so many influential articles and books about the law even while busy deciding cases. Books like *A Matter of Interpretation* and *Reading Law* that are sure to find wide audiences for years to come.

But tonight I want to touch on a more thematic point and suggest that perhaps the great project of Justice Scalia's career was to remind us of the differences between judges and legislators. To remind us that legislators may appeal to their own moral convictions and to claims about social utility to reshape the law as they think it should be in the future. But that judges should do none of these things in a democratic society. That judges should instead strive (if humanly and so imperfectly) to apply the law as it is, focusing backward, not forward, and looking to text, structure, and history to decide what a reasonable reader at the time of the events in question would have understood the law to be—not to decide cases based on their own moral convictions or the policy consequences they believe might serve society best. As Justice Scalia put it, "[i]f you're going to be a good and faithful judge, you have to resign yourself to the fact that you're not always going to like the conclusions you reach. If you like them all the time, you're probably doing something wrong."

It seems to me there can be little doubt about the success of this great project. We live in an age when the job of the federal judge is not so much to expound upon the common law as it is to interpret texts—whether constitutional, statutory, regulatory, or contractual. And as Justice Kagan acknowledged in her Scalia Lecture at Harvard Law School last year, "we're all textualists now." Capturing the spirit of law school back when she and I attended, Justice Kagan went on to relate how professors and students often used to approach reading a statute with the question "[G]osh, what should this statute be," rather than "[W]hat do the words on the paper say?"—in the process wholly conflating the role of the judge with the role of the legislator. Happily, that much has changed, giving way to a return to a much more traditional view of the judicial function, one in which judges seek to interpret texts as reasonable affected parties might have done rather than rewrite texts to suit their own policy preferences. And, as Justice Kagan said, "Justice Scalia had more to do with this [change] than anybody" because he "taught" (or really reminded) "everybody how to do statutory interpretation differently." And one might add: correctly.

I don't think there is any better illustration of Justice Kagan's point than the very first opinion the Supreme Court issued after Justice Scalia's passing. That case—*Lockhart v. United States*—involved the question how best to interpret a statute imposing heightened penalties for three types of offenses—"[1] aggravated sexual abuse, [2] sexual abuse," and "[3] abusive sexual conduct involving a minor or ward." The majority opinion by Justice Sotomayor relied on the rule of the last antecedent and held that the phrase at the end of the sentence—"involving a minor or ward"—modifies only the last offense listed. So that the statute's penalties apply whenever there is aggravated sexual abuse, or sexual abuse, or whenever there is abusive sexual conduct involving a minor or ward. In dissent, Justice Kagan noted that, in "ordinary"

English usage, the rule of the last antecedent bears exceptions and that sometimes a modifying phrase at the end of a sentence reaches further back to earlier antecedents too. And, in Justice Kagan's estimation, an ordinary and average reader of the language at issue here would have thought the phrase "involving a minor or ward" does just that, modifying not just its immediate but all three of its antecedents. So for the statutory penalties to apply, Justice Kagan argued, the government must always prove some kind of sexual abuse involving a minor. In support of her suggestion that an exception rather than the rule should apply to this particular statutory language, Justice Kagan offered this gem of an analogy: "Imagine a friend told you that she hoped to meet 'an actor, director, or producer involved with the new Star Wars movie.' You would know immediately that she wanted to meet an actor from the Star Wars cast—not an actor in, for example, the latest Zoolander." So too here, the Justice reasoned.

As you can see, the two sides in *Lockhart* disagreed pretty avidly and even colorfully. But notice, too, neither appealed to its views of optimal social policy or what the statute "should be." Their dispute focused instead on grammar, language, and statutory structure and on what a reasonable reader in the past would have taken the statute to mean—on what "the words on the paper say." In fact, I have no doubt several Justices found themselves voting for an outcome they would have rejected as legislators. Now, one thing we know about Justice Scalia is that he loved a good fight—and it might be that he loved best of all a fight like this one, over the grammatical effect of a participial phrase. If the Justices were in the business of offering homages instead of judgments, it would be hard to imagine a more fitting tribute to their colleague than this. Surely when the Court handed down its dueling textualist opinions the Justice sat smiling from some happy place.

But of course every worthwhile endeavor attracts its critics. And Justice Scalia's project is no exception. The critics come from different directions and with different agendas. Professor Ronald Dworkin, for example, once called the idea that judges should faithfully apply the law as written an "empty statement" because many legal documents like the Constitution cannot be applied "without making controversial judgments of political morality in the light of [the judge's] own political principles." My admirable colleague, Judge Richard Posner, has also proven a skeptic. He has said it's "naive" to think judges actually believe everything they say in their own opinions; for they often deny the legislative dimension of their work, yet the truth is judges must and should consult their own moral convictions or consequentialist assessments when resolving hard cases. Immediately after Justice Scalia's death, too, it seemed so many more added their voices to the choir. Professor Laurence Tribe, for one, wrote admiringly of the Justice's contributions to the law. But he tempered his admiration by seemingly chastising the Justice for having focused too much on the means by which judicial decisions should be made and not enough on results, writing that "interpretive methods" don't "determine, much less eclipse, outcome[s]."

Well, I'm afraid you'll have to mark me down as naive, a believer that empty statements can bear content, and an adherent to the view that outcomes (ends) do not justify methods (means). Respectfully, it seems to me an assiduous focus on text, structure, and history is essential to the proper exercise of the judicial function. That, yes, judges should be in the business of declaring what the law is using the traditional tools of interpretation, rather than pronouncing the law as they might wish it to be in light of their own political views, always with an eye on the outcome, and engaged perhaps in some Benthamite calculation of pleasures and pains along the way. Though the critics are loud and the temptations to join them may be many, mark me down too as a believer that the traditional account of the judicial role Justice Scalia defended will endure. Let me offer you tonight three reasons for my faith on this score.

FIRST, CONSIDER THE CONSTITUTION. Judges, after all, must do more than merely consider it. They take an oath to uphold it. So any theory of judging (in this country at least) must be measured against that foundational duty. Yet it seems to me those who would have judges behave like legislators, imposing their moral convictions and utility calculi on others, face an uphill battle when it comes to reconciling their judicial philosophy with our founding document.

Consider what happened at the constitutional convention. There the framers expressly debated a proposal that would have incorporated the judiciary into a "council of revision" with sweeping powers to review and veto congressional legislation. A proposal that would have afforded judges the very sorts of legislative powers that some of Justice Scalia's critics would have them assume now. But that proposal went down to defeat at the hands of those who took the traditional view that judges should expound upon the law only as it comes before them, free from the bias of having participated in its creation and from the burden of having to decide "the policy of public measures." In place of a system that mixed legislative and judicial powers, the framers quite deliberately chose one that carefully separated them.

The Constitution itself reflects this choice in its very design, devoting distinct articles to the "legislative Power" and the "judicial Power," creating separate institutions for each, and treating those powers in contradistinction. Neither were these separate categories empty ones to the founding generation. Informed by a hard-earned intellectual inheritance—one perhaps equal parts English common law experience and Enlightenment philosophy—the founders understood the legislative power as the power to prescribe new rules of general applicability for the future. A power properly guided by the will of the people acting through their representatives, a task avowedly political in nature, and one unbound by the past except to the extent that any piece of legislation must of course conform to the higher law of the Constitution itself.

Meanwhile, the founders understood the judicial power as a very different kind of power. Not a forward-looking but a backward-looking authority. Not a way for making new rules of general applicability but a means for resolving disputes about what existing law is and how it applies to discrete cases and controversies. A necessary incident to civil society to be sure but a distinct one. One that calls for neutral arbiters, not elected representatives. One that employs not utility calculi but analogies to past precedents to resolve current disputes. And a power constrained by its dependence on the adversarial system to identify the issues and arguments for decision—a feature of the judicial power that generally means the scope of any rule of decision will be informed and bounded by the parties' presentations rather than only by the outer limits of the judicial imagination. As the founders understood it, the task of the judge is to interpret and apply the law as a reasonable and reasonably well-informed citizen might have done when engaged in the activity underlying the case or controversy—not to amend or revise the law in some novel way. As Blackstone explained, the job of the judge in a government of separated powers is not to "make" or "new-model" the law. Or as Hamilton later echoed, it is for the judiciary to exercise "neither FORCE nor WILL, but merely judgment." Or again, as Marshall put it, it is for the judiciary to say (only) "what the law is."

So many specific features of the Constitution confirm what its larger structure suggests. For example, if the founders really thought legislators free to judge and judges free to legislate, why would they have gone to such trouble to limit the sweep of legislative authority—to insist that it pass through the arduous process of bicameralism and presentment—only to entrust judges to perform the same essential function without similar safeguards? And why would they have insisted on legislators responsive to the people but then allowed judges to act as legislators without similar accountability? Why, too, would they have devised a system that permits equally unrepresentative litigants to define the scope of debate over new legislation based on their narrow self-interest? And if judges were free to legislate new rules of general applicability for the future, why would the founders have considered precedent as among the primary tools of the judicial trade rather than more forward-looking instruments like empirical data? And why would they have entrusted such decisions to a single judge, or even a few judges, aided only by the latest crop of evanescent law clerks, rather than to a larger body with more collective expertise?

In response to observations like these, Judge Posner has replied that "American appellate courts are councils of wise elders and it is not *completely insane* to entrust them with responsibility for deciding cases in a way that will produce the best results" for society. But, respectfully, even that's not exactly a ringing endorsement of judges as social utility optimizers, is it? I can think of a lot of things that aren't *completely* insane but still distinctly ill-advised (or so I try to convince my teenage daughters). And, respectfully too, wouldn't we have to be at least a little crazy to recognize the Constitution's separation of judicial and legislative powers, and the duty of judges to uphold it, but then applaud when judges ignore all that to pursue what they have divined to be the best policy outcomes? And crazy not to worry that if judges consider themselves free to disregard the Constitution's separation of powers they might soon find other bothersome parts of the Constitution equally unworthy of their fidelity?

THIS FIRST POINT LEADS to a second. It seems to me that the separation of legislative and judicial powers isn't just a formality dictated by the Constitution. Neither is it just about ensuring that two institutions with basically identical functions are balanced one against the other. To the founders, the legislative and judicial powers were distinct by nature and their separation was among the most important liberty-protecting devices of the constitutional design, an independent right of the people essential to the preservation of all other rights later enumerated in the Constitution and its amendments. Though much could be said on this subject, tonight permit me to suggest a few reasons why recognizing, defending, and yes policing, the legislative-judicial divide is critical to preserving other constitutional values like due process, equal protection, and the guarantee of a republican form of government.

Consider if we allowed the legislator to judge. If legislatures were free to act as courts and impose their decisions retroactively, they would be free to punish individuals for completed conduct they're unable to alter. And to do so without affording affected individuals any of the procedural protections that normally attend the judicial process. Raising along the way serious due process questions: after all, how would a citizen ever have fair notice of the law or be able to order his or her affairs around it if the lawmaker could go back in time and outlaw retroactively what was reasonably thought lawful at the time? With due process concerns like these would come equal protection problems, too. If legislators could routinely act retroactively, what would happen to disfavored groups and individuals? With their past actions known and unalterable, they would seem easy targets for discrimination. No doubt worries like these are exactly why the founders were so emphatic that legislation should generally bear only prospective effect—proscribing bills of attainder and ex post facto laws criminalizing completed conduct—and why baked into the "legislative Power" there's a presumption as old as the common law that *all* legislation, whether criminal or civil, touches only future, not past, conduct. ("'Every tin horn dictator in the world today, every president for life, has a Bill of Rights,' said Scalia. . . . 'That's not what makes us free; if it did, you would rather live in Zimbabwe. But you wouldn't want to live in most countries in the world that have a Bill of Rights. What has made us free is our Constitution. Think of the word "constitution;" it means structure.' . . . 'The genius of the American constitutional system is the dispersal of power,' he said. 'Once power is centralized in one person, or one part [of government], a Bill of Rights is just words on paper.'")

Now consider the converse situation, if we allowed the judge to act like a legislator. Unconstrained by the bicameralism and presentment hurdles of Article I, the judge would need only his own vote, or those of just a few colleagues, to revise the law willy-nilly in accordance with his preferences and the task of legislating would become a relatively simple thing. Notice, too, how hard it would be to revise this so easily made judicial legislation to account for changes in the world or to fix mistakes. Unable to throw judges out of office in regular elections, you'd have to wait for them to die before you'd have any chance of change. And even then you'd find change difficult, for courts cannot so easily undo their errors given the weight they afford precedent. Notice finally how little voice the people would be left in a government where life-appointed judges are free to legislate alongside elected representatives. The very idea of self-government would seem to wither to the point of pointlessness. Indeed, it seems that for reasons just like these Hamilton explained that "liberty can have nothing to fear from the judiciary alone," but that it "ha[s] every thing to fear from [the] union" of the judicial and legislative powers. Blackstone painted an even grimmer picture of a world in which judges were free to legislate, suggesting that there "men would be[come] slaves to their magistrates."

In case you think the founders' faith in the liberty-protecting qualities of the separation of powers is too ancient to be taken seriously, let me share with you the story of Alfonzo De Niz Robles. Mr. De Niz Robles is a Mexican citizen, married to a U.S. citizen, and the father of four U.S. citizens. In 1999, he agreed to depart the country after being apprehended by immigration authorities. For two years his wife tried without luck to secure him a spousal visa. At that point, Mr. De Niz Robles decided to return to the United States and try his own luck at applying for lawful residency. In doing so, though, he faced two competing statutory provisions that confused his path. One appeared to require him to stay outside the country for at least a decade before applying for admission because of his previous unlawful entry. Another seemed to suggest the Attorney General could overlook this past transgression and adjust his residency status immediately. In 2005, my colleagues took up the question how to reconcile these two apparently competing directions. In the end, the Tenth Circuit held that the latter provision controlled and the Attorney General's adjustment authority remained intact. And it was precisely in reliance on this favorable judicial interpretation that Mr. De Niz Robles filed his application for relief.

But then a curious thing happened. The Board of Immigration Appeals (BIA) issued a ruling that purported to disagree with and maybe even overrule our 2005 decision, one holding that immigrants like Mr. De Niz Robles cannot apply for an immediate adjustment of status and must instead always satisfy the ten-year waiting period. In support of its view on this score, the BIA argued that the statutory scheme was ambiguous, that under *Chevron* step 2 it enjoyed the right to exercise its own "delegated legislative judgment," that as a matter of policy it preferred a different approach, and that it could enforce its new policy retroactively to individuals like Mr. De Niz Robles. So that, *and* quite literally, an *executive* agency acting in a faux-*judicial* proceeding and exercising delegated *legislative* authority purported to overrule an existing *judicial* declaration about the meaning of existing law and apply its new *legislative* rule retroactively to already completed conduct. Just describing what happened here might be enough to make James Madison's head spin.

What did all this mixing of what should be separated powers mean for due process and equal protection values? After our decision in 2005, Mr. De Niz Robles thought the law gave him a choice: begin a ten-year waiting period outside the country or apply for relief immediately. In reliance on a judicial declaration of the law as it was, he unsurprisingly chose the latter option. Then when it turned to his case in 2014, the BIA ruled that that option was no option at all. Telling him, in essence, that he'd have to start the decade-long clock now—even though if he'd known back in 2005 that this was his only option, his wait would be almost over. So it is that, after a man relied on a judicial declaration of what the law was, an agency in an adjudicatory proceeding sought to make a legislative policy decision with retroactive effect, in full view of and able to single out winners and losers, penalizing an individual for conduct he couldn't alter, and denying him any chance to conform his conduct to a legal rule knowable in advance.

What does this story suggest? That combining what are by design supposed to be separate and distinct legislative and judicial powers poses a grave threat to our values of personal liberty, fair notice, and equal protection. And that the problem isn't just one of King George's time but one that persists even today, during the reign of King James (LeBron, that is).

★

AT THIS POINT I can imagine the critic replying this way. Sure, judges should look to the traditional tools of text, structure, history, and precedent. But in hard cases those materials will prove indeterminate. So *some* tiebreaker is needed, and that's where the judge's political convictions, a consequentialist calculus, or something else must and should come into play.

Respectfully, though, I'd suggest to you the critics' conclusion doesn't follow from their premise. If anything, replies along these lines seem to me to wind up supplying a third and independent reason for embracing the traditional view of judging: it compares favorably to the offered alternatives.

Now, I do not mean to suggest that traditional legal tools will yield a single definitive right answer in every case. Of course Ronald Dworkin famously thought otherwise, contending that a Herculean judge could always land on the right answer. But at least in my experience most of us judges don't much resemble Hercules—there's a reason we wear loose-fitting robes—and I accept the possibility that some hard cases won't lend themselves to a clear right answer.

At the same time, though, I'd suggest to you that the amount of indeterminacy in the law is often (wildly) exaggerated. Law students are fed a steady diet of hard cases in overlarge and overly costly casebooks

stuffed with the most vexing and difficult appellate opinions ever issued. Hard cases are, as well, the daily bread of the professoriate and a
source of riches for the more perfumed advocates in our profession. But
I wonder: somewhere along the way did anyone ever share with you
the fact that only 5.6% of federal lawsuits make it all the way to decision in an appellate court? Or that, even among the small sliver of cases
that make it so far, over 95% are resolved unanimously by the courts
of appeals? Or that, even when it comes to the very hardest cases that
remain, the cases where circuit judges do disagree and the Supreme
Court grants certiorari, all nine Justices are able to resolve them unanimously about 40% of the time? The fact is, over 360,000 cases are filed
every year in our federal courts. Yet in the Supreme Court, a Justice
voices dissent in only about 50 cases per year. My law clerks reliably
inform me that's about 0.014% of all cases. Focusing on the hard cases
may be fun, but doesn't it risk missing the forest for the trees?

And doesn't it also risk missing the *reason* why such a remarkable
percentage of cases *are* determined by existing legal rules? The truth is
that the traditional tools of legal analysis do a remarkable job of elimi-
nating or reducing indeterminacy. Yes, lawyers and judges may sometimes disagree about which canons of construction are most helpful in
the art of ascertaining Congress's meaning in a complicated statute. We
may sometimes disagree over the order of priority we should assign to
competing canons. And sometimes we may even disagree over the results they yield in particular cases. But when judges pull from the same
toolbox and look to the same materials to answer the same narrow
question—what might a reasonable person have thought the law was
at the time—we confine the range of possible outcomes and provide a
remarkably stable and predictable set of rules people are able to follow.
And even when a hard case does arise, once it's decided it takes on the

force of precedent, becomes an easy case in the future, and contributes further to the determinacy of our law. Truly the system is a wonder and it is little wonder so many throughout the world seek to emulate it.

Besides, it seems to me that even accepting some hard cases remain—maybe something like that 0.014%—it just doesn't follow that we must or should resort to our own political convictions, consequentialist calculi, or any other extra-legal rule of decision to resolve them. Just as Justices Sotomayor and Kagan did in *Lockhart*, we can make our decisions based on a comparative assessment of the various legal clues—choosing whether the rule of the last antecedent or one of its exceptions best fits the case in light of the particular language at hand. At the end of the day, we may not be able to claim confidence that there's a certain and single right answer to every case, but there's no reason why we cannot make our best judgment depending on (and only on) conventional legal materials, relying on a sort of closed record if you will, without peeking to outside evidence. No reason, too, why we cannot conclude for ourselves that one side has the better of it, even if by a nose, and even while admitting that a disagreeing colleague could see it the other way. As Justice Scalia once explained, "[e]very canon is simply *one indication* of meaning; and if there are more contrary indications (perhaps supported by other canons), it must yield. But that does not render the entire enterprise a fraud—not, at least, unless the judge wishes to make it so."

Neither do I see the critics as offering a better alternative. Consider a story Justice Scalia loved to tell. Imagine two men walking in the woods who happen upon an angry bear. They start running for their lives. But the bear is quickly gaining on them. One man yells to the other, "We'll never be able to outrun this bear!" The other replies calmly, "I don't have to outrun the bear, I just have to outrun you." As Justice Scalia explained, just because the traditional view of judging may not yield a single right answer in all hard cases doesn't mean we should or must abandon it. The real question is whether the critics can offer anything better.

About that, I have my doubts. Take the model of the judge as pragmatic social-welfare maximizer. In that model, judges purport to weigh the costs and benefits associated with the various possible outcomes of the case at hand and pick the outcome best calculated to maximize our collective social welfare. But in hard cases don't *both* sides usually have a pretty persuasive story about how deciding in their favor would advance the social good? In criminal cases, for example, we often hear arguments from the government that its view would promote public security or finality. Meanwhile, the defense often tells us that its view would promote personal liberty or pro-cedural fairness. How is a judge supposed to weigh or rank these radically different social goods? The fact is the pragmatic model of judging offers us no *value* or *rule* for determining which costs and ben-efits are to be preferred and we are left only with a radically under-determined choice to make. It's sort of like being asked to decide which is better, the arrival of Hue Jackson or the return of LeBron James? Both may seem like pretty good things to the Cleveland sports fan, but they are incommensurate goods, and unless you introduce some special rule or metric there's no way to say for certain which is to be preferred. In just this way, it seems to me that at the end of the day the critics who would have us trade in the traditional account of judging for one that focuses on social utility optimization would only have us trade in one sort of indeterminacy problem for another. And the indeterminacy problem invited by the critics may well be a good deal more problematic given the challenges of trying to square their model of judging with our constitutional design and its underlying values. So before we throw overboard our traditional views about the separation of the judicial and legislative roles, it seems to me we might all do well to remember The Bear.

★

WITH THE THREE POINTS I've briefly sketched here tonight, I hope I've given you some sense why I believe Justice Scalia's vision of the "good and faithful judge" is a worthy one. But so far I've discussed mostly principle, not experience. And I run the risk of an objection from those who might suggest that there's more in heaven and earth than is dreamt of in my philosophy. So, as I close, I want to make plain that the traditional account of law and judging not only makes the most sense to me as an intellectual matter, it also makes the most sense of my own lived experience in the law.

My days and years in our shared professional trenches have taught me that the law bears its own distinctive structure, language, coherence, and integrity. When I was a lawyer and my young daughter asked me what lawyers do, the best I could come up with was to say that lawyers help people solve their problems. As simple as it is, I still think that's about right. Lawyers take on their clients' problems as their own; they worry and lose sleep over them; they struggle mightily to solve them. They do so with a respect for and in light of the law as it is, seeking to make judgments about the future based on a set of reasonably stable existing rules. That is not politics by another name: that is the ancient and honorable practice of law.

Now as I judge I see too that donning a black robe means something—and not just that I can hide the coffee stains on my shirts. We wear robes—honest, unadorned, black polyester robes that we (yes) are expected to buy for ourselves at the local uniform supply store— as a reminder of what's expected of us when we go about our business: what Burke called the "cold neutrality of an impartial judge."

Throughout my decade on the bench, I have watched my colleagues strive day in and day out to do just as Socrates said we should—to hear courteously, answer wisely, consider soberly, and decide impartially. Men and women who do not thrust themselves into the limelight but who tend patiently and usually quite obscurely to the great promise of our legal system—the promise that all litigants, rich or poor, mighty or meek, will receive equal protection under the law and due process for their grievance. Judges who assiduously seek to avoid the temptation to secure results they prefer. And who do, in fact, regularly issue judgments with which they disagree as a matter of policy—all because they think that's what the law fairly demands.

Justice Scalia's defense of this traditional understanding of our professional calling is a legacy every person in this room has now inherited. And it is one you students will be asked to carry on and pass down soon enough. I remember as if it were yesterday sitting in a law school audience like this one. Listening to a newly minted Justice Scalia offer his Oliver Wendell Holmes lecture titled "The Rule of Law as a Law of Rules." He offered that particular salvo in his defense of the traditional view of judging and the law almost thirty years ago now. It all comes so quickly. But it was and remains, I think, a most worthy way to spend a life.

May he rest in peace.

Notes

2   "You saw a very well planned out": "How Trump Picked Supreme Court Nominee Neil Gorsuch," Eric Spillman, CNN wire, February 1, 2017.

2   Senate Minority Leader Chuck Schumer called him an "ideologue": "Schumer: Democrats will filibuster Gorsuch nomination": Robert Barnes, Ed O'Keefe, and Ann E. Marimow, *Washington Post*, March 23, 2017.

3   One commentator wrote: "The Conservative pipeline to the Supreme Court," Jeffrey Toobin, *The New Yorker*, April 17, 2017.

3   The morning after the hearings opened: "Supreme Court Nominee Neil Gorsuch's First Day of Hearings," Robert Barnes, Ed O'Keefe, and Sean Sullivan, *Washington Post*, March 20, 2017.

9   In a 2004 tribute: "Six of the Greatest," Ben S. Aisenberg, *The Colorado Lawyer*, May 2004.

11 Shortly after the president nominated Gorsuch: "Simply Stated, Gorsuch Is . . ." Kimberly Kindy, Sari Horwitz, and William Wan, *Washington Post*, February 18, 2017.

20 Dr. Steven Ochs recalls: Author interview, April 11, 2017.

22 Tom Conlan remembers that: Author interview, April 13, 2017.

23 Jonathan Brody, one of his closest childhood friends: Kindy, Horwitz, and Wan.

25 For example, in late February 2017: "Neil Gorsuch's Late Mother Almost Annihilated the EPA," *Newsweek*, February 1, 2017.

27 When the White House lawyers came to Burford: *Are You Tough Enough?* Anne Burford with John Greenya, McGraw-Hill, 1986.

30 "Joe wants to see you: *Ibid.*

31 In the unlikely event: *Ibid.*

36 Shortly after Gorsuch was nominated: "Class of '91, Obama and Gorsuch Rubbed Shoulders at . . ." Joanna Walters, *The Guardian*, February 5, 2017.

45 Barack Obama decided to go home to Chicago: "The Crazy Reason Why Barack Obama Didn't Want to Be a Supreme Court Clerk," Staci Zaretsky, *Above the Law*, May 26, 2017.

47 Some of John Finnis's views are very controversial: "Neil Gorsuch had a tense exchange," Tessa Berenson, *Time*, March 21, 2017.

48 After graduating from Oxford: *The Future of Assisted Suicide and Euthanasia*, Neil M. Gorsuch, Princeton University Press, 2006.

49 But at the time of his confirmation: "Neil Gorsuch writings reveal his support for Coors . . ." Monte Whaley, *Denver Post*, February 12, 2017.

54 Todd C. Peppers, who teaches at Roanoke College: "How Gorsuch the Clerk Met Kennedy the Justice," Adam Liptak and Nicholas Fandos, *New York Times*, February 3, 2017.

55 Each year the Court receives thousands of petitions: "Neil Gorsuch the Law Clerk," Matt Walsh, *SCOTUSblog*, February 24, 2017.

61 "He took a shine to me": "Supreme Clerks," John Greenya, *Washington Lawyer*, May–June 1992.

62 "The Supreme Court clerk of today": *Ibid.*

71 "Neil went to Oxford": "Simply Stated, Gorsuch Is . . .", Kindy, Horwitz, and Wan.

74 One Gorsuch relative: "Supreme Court Pick Neil Gorsuch's stepmother breaks . . . family silence," *Daily Mail*, February 3, 2017.

86 Attorney Wan Kim: Wan Kim, author interview, July 25, 2017.

101 Also serving with Gorsuch: Lily Fu Claffee, author interview, July 25, 2017.

106 Reporting for *Law360*: "The Rocky Road to the Confirmation of Judge Neil Gorsuch," Michael Macagnone, *Law 360*, April 7, 2017.

108 The *Law360* article continues: *Ibid.*

117 On March 22, 2017, *New York Daily News* reporter: "Neil Gorsuch Questioned About Role in Bush Administration," *New York Daily News*, March 22, 2017.

122 One of those lawyers was Baine Kerr: Author interview, March 24, 2017.

125 "He had been on the court": *Ibid.*

126 "I think I was up there": *Ibid.*

130 Not surprisingly, Mr. O'Rourke has a clear and vivid memory: Author interview, April 17, 2017.

130 Would Patrick O'Rourke agree: *Ibid.*

138 On February 1: "What Gorsuch's Old Newspaper Columns Say about Him," Amy Wang, *Washington Post*, February 1, 2017.

139 "[H]e criticized protesters": Ibid.

146 "The Hatch Valley may be to chiles": "Gorsuch's Opening Words Speak Volumes About His Style," Stan Parker, *Law 360*, February 1, 2017.

153 Former O'Connor clerk David Kravitz: "Why we should ignore Scalia's nasty zingers," David Kravitz, *Washington Post*, July 31, 2015.

154 Paul Anthony, a longtime television and radio: Author interview, June 30, 2017.

154 Chuck Conconi is another: Author interview, September 6, 2017.

155 In an article headed: "Neil Gorsuch's conservatism is different from Antonin Scalia's," *The Economist*, March 23, 2017.

157 Veteran National Public Radio: "Neil Gorsuch Votes 100 Percent of the Time with Most Conservative Justice," NPR, July 1, 2017.

161 On February 1, George F. Will: there is no philosophizing in the Constitution: George Will, *Washington Post*, February 1, 2017.

163 In it, he expressed his opinion: Charles Schumer, "We Won't Be Fooled Again," *New York Times*, February 10, 2017.

164 "unlikely selection": "Ayotte to Lead White House team . . ." Philip Rucker and Ashley Parker, *Washington Post*, January 31, 2017.

165 "We changed the Senate rules": "Harry Reid . . . ," *New York Times*, December 8, 2016.

168 "Whereas in the fall of 1980": "Hart Building Opens Under Protest," United States Senate, November 22, 1982.

169 "a threat to our American values": Shannon Young. *Masslife*, February 1, 2017.

169 "Our political views span the spectrum": "Former Law Clerks Herald Supreme Court Nominee Neil Gorsuch's Independence," Richard Wolf, *USA Today*, February 14, 2017.

171 "To this senator": Chuck Grassley, "Grassley Statement at a Hearing on the Nomination of Neil Gorsuch to Serve as Associate Justice of the Supreme Court," March 20, 2017.

173 "part of a Republican strategy": "Durbin Calls Gorsuch Nomination . . . ," Peter Stevenson, *Washington Post*, March 20, 2017.

174 "Under the rules": "Judge Gorsuch and the Frozen Truck Driver," Paul Callan, CNN, March 21, 2017.

191 When, on April 7, 2017, Neil: Siraj Hashmi, "Scotus Frat? Neil Gorsuch to get hazed," redalertpolitics.com, April 10, 2017.

193 In an article headed: "Neil Gorsuch Sounded A Lot Like Justice Scalia On His First Day On The Job," Cristian Farias, *Huffington Post*, March 17, 2017.

196 Gorsuch stayed silent for all of ten minutes: "Bitter fight behind him, Gorsuch starts day with relish," Adam Liptak, *New York Times*, April 17, 2017.

198 According to the *New York Times*: "Amidst protests at Trump Hotel, Neil Gorsuch calls for civility," Adam Liptak, *New York Times*, September 28, 2017.

199 And in *Above the Law*: "Judge Gorsuch on the campaign trail," Kathryn Rubino, *Above the Law*, September 27, 2017.

Bibliography

Aisenberg, Ben S., "Six of the Greatest," *Colorado Lawyer*, May 2004.

Anthony, Paul, Author interview, June 30, 2017.

Barnes, Robert, Edward O'Keefe and Sean Sullivan, "Supreme Court Nominee Neil Gorsuch's First Day of Hearings," *Washington Post*, March 20, 2017.

Berenson, Tessa, "Neil Gorsuch Had a Tense Exchange Over Maternity Leave at His Confirmation Hearing," *Time*, March 21, 2017.

Burford, Anne, with John Greenya, *Are You Tough Enough?* McGraw-Hill, 1986.

Callan, Paul, "Judge Gorsuch and the Frozen Truck Driver," CNN, March 21, 2017.

Conconi, Chuck, Author interview, September 6, 2017.

Conlan, Thomas, Author interview, April 13, 2017.

Clafee, Lily Fu, Author interview, July 25, 2017.

Daily Mail, "Supreme Court Pick Neil Gorsuch's Family Breaks Silence," February 2, 2017.

Economist, "Neil Gorsuch's Conservatism Is Different from Antonin Scalia's," July 26, 2017.

Farias, Cristian, "Neil Gorsuch Sounded A Lot Like Justice Scalia On His First Day On The Job,"*Huffington Post*, March 17, 2017.

Gorsuch, Neil, *The Future of Assisted Suicide and Euthanasia*, Princeton University Press, 2006.

Grassley, Charles, "Grassley Statement at a Hearing on the Nomination of Neil Gorsuch to Serve as Associate Justice of the Supreme Court," March 20, 2017.

Greenya, John, with Anne Burford, *Are You Tough Enough?* McGraw-Hill, 1986.

————, "Supreme Clerks," *Washington Lawyer*, May/June 1992.

Hashmi, Siraj, "Scotus Frat? Neil Gorsuch to get hazed," redalertpolitics.com, April 10, 2017.

Horowitz, Sari, with Kimberly Kindy and William Wan, *Washington Post*, February 18, 2017.

Kerr, Baine, Author interview, March 24, 2017.

Kim, Wan, Author interview, July 25, 2017.

Liptak, Adam, "How Gorsuch the Clerk Met Kennedy the Justice," Adam Liptak and Nicholas Fandos, *New York Times*, February 3, 2017.

Lovelace, Ryan, "Liberal group: Gorsuch a 'disastrous' choice for Supreme Court," *Washington Examiner*, January 31, 2017.

Macagnone, Michael, "The Rocky Road to the Confirmation of Judge Neil Gorsuch," *Law360*, April 7, 2017.

New York Daily News, "Neil Gorsuch Questioned About Role in Bush Administration," March 22, 2017.

Newsweek, "Neil Gorsuch's Late Mother Almost Annihilated the EPA," February 1, 2017.

Ochs, Steven, Author interview, April 11, 2017.

O'Rourke, Patrick, Author interview, April 17, 2017.

Parker, Ashley, with Philip Rucker, "Ayotte to lead White House team," *Washington Post*, January 24, 2017.

Parker, Stan, "Gorsuch's Opening Words Speak Volumes About His Style," *Law360*, February 1, 2017.

Peltz, Jennifer, "At Liberal Columbia U. Gorsuch Raised a Conservative Voice," Associated Press, February 5, 2017.

Peppers, Todd, with Artemus Ward (editors), *In Chambers: Stories of Supreme Court Law Clerks and Their Clerks*, University of Virginia Press, 2012.

Reid, Harry, "We changed the Senate rules," *New York Times*, December 8, 2016.

Rucker, Philip, with Ashley Parker, "Ayotte to lead White House team," *Washington Post*, January 24, 2017.

Schumer, Charles, "We Won't Be Fooled Again," *New York Times*, February 10, 2017.

Spillman, Eric, "How Trump Picked Supreme Court Nominee Neil Gorsuch," CNN wire, February 1, 2017.

Stevenson, Peter, "Durbin calls Gorsuch nomination 'part of a Republican strategy to capture our judicial branch,'" *Washington Post*, March 20, 2017.

Toobin, Jeffrey, "The Conservative pipeline to the Supreme Court," *The New Yorker*, April 17, 2017.

Totenberg, Nina, "Neil Gorsuch Votes 100 Percent of the Time with Most Conservative Justice," *National Public Radio*, July 1, 2017.

United States Senate, "Hart Building Opens Under Protest," November 22, 1892.

Walters, Joanna, "Class of '91: Obama and Gorsuch rubbed shoulders at Harvard, but their paths split," *The Guardian*, February 5, 2017.

Wang, Amy, "What Gorsuch's old newspaper columns say about him," *Washington Post*, February 1, 2017.

Whaley, Monte, "Neil Gorsuch writings reveal his support for Coors . . . ," *Denver Post*, February 12, 2017.

Will, George, "There is no philosophizing in the Constitution," *Washington Post*, February 1, 2017.

Wolf, Richard, "Former Law Clerks Herald Supreme Court Nominee Neil Gorsuch's Independence," *USA Today*, February 14, 2017.

Young, Shannon, "President Donald Trump picks Appellate Judge Neil Gorsuch for US Supreme Court nominee," *Masslive*, February 1, 2017.

Zaretsky, Staci, "The Crazy Reason Why Barack Obama Didn't Want to be a Supreme Court Clerk," *Above the Law*, May 26, 2017.

Acknowledgments

Thanks first to my Threshold editor, Natasha Simons, for fair commentary and judicious editing from beginning to end; to her able assistant, Hannah Brown; to Steve Troha of the Folio Literary Management, and especially to his colleague and my original agent, Jeffrey Kleinman, who pitched in at the very end to guarantee that I made my already stretched deadline. (In the writing of some two dozen books, I've never before had an agent who put so much time and effort into helping finish the book.)

Next, thanks go to friends and family for their support and encouragement: various Greenyas—Bob, Jim, Tim, Kris, Bobby and Mare, and Genie Greenya Teter; Jeff Teter for dinner in Denver, among other favors, and his father, Jim Teter; hometown friends Andy Clarke, Bill McCarty, Lou (and Honey) Patscot, Don Gral, Joe Heil, Ray Laub, Mary Stevens Fuller, Tim Cowdin, Jim Boyce, Tom Cincotta and his sister-in-law Nancy S. Cincotta, and, most especially, my favorite Christian, Christian ("Chris") Harwich, journalist-turned-lawyer-turned-public-defender, for advice and support on many fronts. Special thanks to my grandchildren Samantha ("Sammy") Greenya, who worked on the book during her first college summer, and her sister and brother, Alexandra ("Lexy") and Will.

Thanks also to far-flung friends John Florescu (Bucharest), Joe Lauria (New York City and Iraq), Californians Jim Dunn, Peter and Roz Bonerz, and Charlie Siebert and his son Chris, Bob, and Anne Ganz (Martha's Vineyard), and Mike Wustner (Bali).

Nearby friends: Herb and Betty Karp, Bud and Connie Hart, Katy Segal, Nick and Mary Lou Kotz, and the gang at Moose Lodge 1695 in Warrenton, Virginia, especially Robin the Reader Woodward, Wayne ("Wanker") Harne and Cindy, and Tom Jacobs; Dr. Anna Hauptman, GWU President Emeritus Steve Trachtenberg, and all the artists at Puglisi's barbershop in Washington, D.C.

Thanks to many lawyers, but especially: F. Lee Bailey, Mahlon Brown, Plato Cacheris, John Crigler, Steve Grafman, Henry Gonzalez, Chris Harwich (again), and Roger Zuckerman.

Thanks to two fine people I met years ago who had worked for and with the late Anne Gorsuch Burford: attorney John Daniel and Cristina ("Cristy") Bach Yeutter.

And, finally, for renting me the most beautiful spot in which to write, the Lady and Lord of Wildcat Mountain (Virginia), Jocylyn ("Lili") Alexander and her fiancé Roland Word.

Index